Living FREE FROM Sin

Volume 1
By Ernest Angley

Living Free From Sin *Volume 1*
All Rights Reserved.
Copyright © 2007 Ernest Angley.
Printed in the United States of America.
Distributed by Winston Press.
P.O. Box 2091, Akron, Ohio 44309

We humbly dedicate this book to a wonderful warrior of the Lord.

This book is dedicated to Maxine Young. She was the editor and reporter for the Ernest Angley Ministries for many years, but she was suddenly called to her heavenly home on August 20, 2007. She was an amazing handmaiden of the Lord – consecrated, dedicated and separated into His grace, faith, and love. She had great vision of this Jesus World Outreach, to win the lost at any cost.

Maxine, you are greatly missed. We will meet you in heaven one wonderful day. You are special to God and to us, and you will always be greatly loved. Thanks for all of your wonderful work.

We'll see you, Maxine, in the morning.

CONTENTS

CHAPTER 1:
Eternal Security — 1

•

CHAPTER 2:
Letters From The Lord — 61

•

CHAPTER 3:
Sin Brings Judgment — 77

•

CHAPTER 4:
The Garments — 93

•

CHAPTER 5:
Ten Commandments — 109

•

CHAPTER 6:
Flesh And The Devil — 141

•

CHAPTER 7:
More Works Of The Flesh — 177

•

CHAPTER 8:
The Deceitfulness Of Sin — 208

•

CHAPTER 9:
Let Romans Put It All Together — 232

•

CHAPTER 10:
Some Final Words To The Romans — 262

CHAPTER 1

Eternal Security

*I*n a divine visitation in 1954 the Lord told me I would have to know the Spirit of God. He also said I would have to know the spirit of the devil and the spirit of man. This book will deal with the spirit of man. When God speaks of man in the Bible, He means woman as well. God is telling us much about man and woman.

I knew that studying the kingdom of the devil, the Kingdom of God and God's ways would be tremendous; but studying man, I thought, would be a small subject. I've learned it's a big subject. God was going to teach me the spirit of people.

Some of you don't understand people because you don't really understand yourself. Your weaknesses color the way you look at others, at their doubts, fears, misgivings and so forth. If you are full of God, however, you find it easy to look at others who are full of God as well and to overlook those who are not; you identify with people who have good thoughts.

IN THE BEGINNING

In all love, grace, goodness, and loving tenderkindness, the Lord gave Adam and Eve this message in the Garden: If you go to the tree of death, you'll die.

Unconditional eternal security claims that a person once saved cannot be lost regardless of what he or she does. The damnable doctrine of unconditional eternal security has raged for years and years. It started in Eden as the lie that beguiled Adam and Eve and caused them to fall from grace, and the devil has spread this damnable doctrine of not being able to live sin-free throughout the Christian world; that's the reason the Christian world has little influence today. *When you don't live free from sin, you don't worship the true and living God, saith the Lord.* You can't worship Him in sin; it is impossible. This doctrine is destroying many, and the Lord is going to use His truth in mighty, mighty ways in this final hour to open eyes.

I find a lot of people are sincere, and a lot of preachers are sincere; but they are sincerely wrong. When I go into a country, the Lord lets me know again and again what their trouble is and why, and the Lord told me that in one particular place it was ignorance; they didn't know any better. Hardly a preacher, if any, believed that Christians have to live absolutely free from all sin. The Lord didn't point out one preacher in the ministers' meeting who believed people could live free from all sin. Some of the laypeople were in better shape than the ministers, yet they, too, were in the darkness of ignorance.

A DAMNABLE DOCTRINE

You can either live free from sin or live in the bondage of sin. Which way does the Bible endorse? Certainly you know the answer. The devil, however, has caused man to take the Holy Scriptures of God, the voice of God, and twist it into all kinds of falsehoods that deceive people. Many declare they're on their way to heaven when, in fact, they're going straight to hell.

We can't study the spirit of man without studying eternal security; we need to know everything about it. Is salvation conditional or unconditional? Unconditional eternal security declares that it is unconditional: Once saved always saved, once in grace always in grace. In Eden, however, you find a man and woman made in the image of God. They were cast out, although with one exception, they had previously lived in perfect grace, in perfect love, in perfect peace, in perfect everything.

Adam and Eve were wonderfully made, their bodies completely healthy. They were to have lived forever just like God the Father, God the Son, and God the Holy Ghost—without one speck of hate or disobedience, without tears, sorrows, or heartaches. But when man sinned, he found that his eternal life in Paradise was conditional. The Lord, in fact, had let Adam and Eve know in the beginning that **of every tree of the garden thou mayest freely eat: But of the tree of the knowledge of good and evil, thou shalt not eat of it: for in the day that thou eatest thereof thou shalt surely die** (Genesis 2:16,17).

Had Adam and Eve stayed away from the tree of death in Eden, they would never have been sick, never had to earn their food by the sweat of their brow, never seen a dead loved one, or never been separated from those they loved. No, they were beautiful in every way, so pure in their thinking and actions that God would come down daily to walk with them. As much as the family in heaven is a part of God, they were a part of God's family and were on their way to living forever in the grace of God. Possessing everything they could have ever longed for, Adam and Eve didn't need banks, securities, or money; all they needed was freely given to them. They were never meant to have one worry. But when man and woman fell from grace, they lost everything; being part of the family of God was all conditional.

THE DANGER OF SERPENT TALK

When you find salvation, you are given eternal life in the grace of God, but it is conditional; it all depends on how you live and act whether or not you get to keep all this greatness—and heaven is included in your gift of salvation. We are promised eternal security, but it's conditional. The devil wants us to believe that no conditions are involved in God's promises. **And the serpent said unto the woman, Ye shall not surely die** (Genesis 3:4). That same old serpent is alive and on planet Earth today telling preachers, priests and teachers alike: *You won't really die! Why, no one can live free from sin. God didn't really mean what He said.*

But God really did mean it. Although the body was made out of the dust of the earth, it is worth more than all the silver and gold in the world. That dust was holy dust; the Lord had put His life into it when He breathed on man and woman and gave them a living soul like His own. What great trust

God put in the man and woman He made! It seems unbelievable that they sinned; yet the story is true.

So he [God] drove out the man; and he placed at the east of the garden of Eden Cherubims, and a flaming sword which turned every way, to keep the way of the tree of life (Genesis 3:24). God put angels by the Garden and a flaming sword that turned in every direction to make it impossible for man and woman in their sinful state to get back into Eden.

STATEMENT NUMBER ONE:
ONCE SAVED THERE WILL BE NO PUNISHMENT

This first statement in favor of unconditional eternal security is based on the false idea that people will not receive future punishment, no matter what. It's based on the hope that God will acquit the wicked even though they have not repented of their sins. Beware of the hope that statement gives you. There is nothing to keep you from being swept away into eternal damnation if one willful sin is in you when you die. Satan is still telling people today: *Thou shalt not surely die!* How sad to see even drunken people, drug addicts, other sinners, and church people so deceived that they claim they're God's children on their way to heaven.

The Bible says no sinner can inherit the Kingdom

of God, and God has the final say. **Know ye not that the unrighteous shall not inherit the kingdom of God? Be not deceived: neither fornicators, nor idolaters, nor adulterers, nor effeminate, nor abusers of themselves with mankind, Nor thieves, nor covetous, nor drunkards, nor revilers, nor extortioners, shall inherit the kingdom of God** (I Corinthians 6:9,10).

Many think that, even though they're disobedient, they're still a child of God because they were once saved. Even the devil-possessed will come into the healing line and tell me they are saved. Can you see how deceiving the devil is? He has fooled many people, teachers, preachers and priests alike, some who were once true believers in Christ.

No one can get into heaven unless that one is sinless through the blood and the pure Word of God. **And the Word** [Jesus Christ] **was made flesh, and dwelt among us, (and we beheld his glory, the glory as of the only begotten of the Father,) full of grace and truth** (John 1:14). Jesus, the living Word, speaks: **I am the door: by me if any man enter in, he shall be saved, and shall go in and out, and find pasture** (John 10:9). Jesus is our door into heaven, but we can only go through that door if we are without sin.

No scripture teaches or even hints that the doctrine

of unconditional eternal security is valid. Unconditional eternal security is one of the most hellish doctrines ever to come forth, full of deceit and deadly promise. This doctrine has damned many souls; the results of this doctrine are completely unacceptable from a moral standpoint. When God says sin can't get into heaven, remember this: It's His heaven, and His Word is the gatekeeper.

This I say then, Walk in the Spirit, and ye shall not fulfil the lust of the flesh (Galatians 5:16). You can't walk in the Spirit unless the love law of Christ is in you. When you walk in the Spirit, you don't fulfill the lust of the flesh; instead, you fulfill the desires of the Holy Spirit Himself. **For the flesh lusteth against the Spirit, and the Spirit against the flesh: and these are contrary the one to the other: so that ye cannot do the things that ye would. But if ye be led of the Spirit, ye are not under the law** (Galatians 5:17,18). After you receive salvation, you're not under the Law of the Old Testament; you're under the sinless Jesus-love law.

Paul lists the fruits of the Holy Spirit that are grown in the hearts and souls of the true born-again Christians. **But the fruit of the Spirit is love, joy, peace, longsuffering, gentleness, goodness, faith, Meekness, temperance: against such there is no law. And they that are Christ's have crucified the** flesh with the affections and lusts. If we live in the Spirit, let us also walk in the Spirit** (Galatians 5:22–25). If you live in the Spirit, you walk in the Spirit—when you are free from all sin.

STATEMENT NUMBER TWO:
GOD'S SHEEP CANNOT STRAY

Another notion of unconditional eternal security is that God's sheep will never perish. **And I give unto them eternal life; and they shall never perish, neither shall any man pluck them out of my hand** (John 10:28). But what does unconditional eternal security do with the prior verse that says, **My sheep hear my voice, and I know them, and they follow me** (John 10:27)? God's sheep have no sin; that's why they follow Jesus. If the devil and all his demons would come at one time against a soul sealed with the blood of Jesus, a soul with no sin, they could not pluck that soul out of the hand of God. The blood seal of redemption by the Holy Spirit Himself protects that pure soul. No one can pluck true children of God out of His hand; but, if they commit sin, they pluck themselves out. God's hand will hold no one who has committed willful sin.

People are deceived by dipping into God's Word and taking out only what they want. The devil uses part of the Word to blind them to what God is really saying. He makes people think he's dipping from God's well, but he isn't dipping from that well because there is no deceit in the well called the Bible. Throughout hundreds of years of dipping in the Word of God, the water has always been—and always will be—pure.

That a person who sins can't be plucked out of God's hand is one of unconditional eternal security's grand thoughts, but it's no thought of God. Didn't God give Adam and Eve eternal life? Yes, He did. There was no shadow of death in Eden when God made the first man and woman, and there was never to have been a shadow of death over a human body—never, never, never. But sin, only one sin, changed all that.

SHEEP CAN GO ASTRAY

Unconditional eternal security teaches that sheep are always sheep, and it is impossible to change them: Once they are God's sheep, they are always God's sheep. But the Bible teaches that if one turns away from God, that one is a lost sheep. If you're lost to God, you're lost to heaven and lost to His love, peace, and joy. You're lost to His teachings, to following Him, and to the knowledge of His voice.

A sheep is lost until it is found. **And he** [Jesus]

spake this parable unto them, saying, What man of you, having an hundred sheep, if he lose one of them, doth not leave the ninety and nine in the wilderness, and go after that which is lost, until he find it? And when he hath found it, he layeth it on his shoulders, rejoicing. And when he cometh home, he calleth together his friends and neighbours, saying unto them, Rejoice with me; for I have found my sheep which was lost. I say unto you, that likewise joy shall be in heaven over one sinner that repenteth, more than over ninety and nine just persons, which need no repentance** (Luke 15:3–7). Jesus is clearly saying that His sheep who have gone astray must repent if they are to come back into His fold.

All we like sheep have gone astray; we have turned every one to his own way; and the LORD hath laid on him the iniquity of us all (Isaiah 53:6). Isaiah is comparing us to sheep who have gone astray, but sin caused us to do it. However, Jesus as our Sacrificial Lamb bore all our iniquities and all our sins, and He will forgive us if we repent with godly sorrow.

When you turn to your own way, it isn't just your way alone; you've actually turned to the devil's way. **There is a way which seemeth right unto a man, but the end thereof are the ways of death**

(Proverbs 14:12). Ministers deceived with this rotten doctrine of unconditional eternal security have preached millions into heaven who were screaming in hell the whole time the funeral was going on. According to the ministers, they have eternal life because once saved always saved, and once in grace always in grace. The truth of God is that those who die with any willful sin at all in their soul are not in heaven; they're in the torments of hell.

For ye were as sheep going astray; but are now returned unto the Shepherd and Bishop of your souls (I Peter 2:25). If you don't have the Keeper of your soul, you're not going to heaven when you die. The blood of Jesus is the keeper of your soul; you must have the blood applied to your soul. The blood will not mix with sin; if you have sin, you don't have the blood. **Therefore to him that knoweth to do good, and doeth it not, to him it is sin** (James 4:17).

TYPES OF CHRIST: A SHEEP AND A GOAT

In the Bible, Christ is typified by both a sheep and a goat: **If a soul commit a trespass, and sin through ignorance, in the holy things of the LORD; then he shall bring for his trespass unto the LORD a ram without blemish out of the flocks, with thy estimation by she-kels of silver, after the shekel** of the sanctuary, for a trespass offering (Leviticus 5:15).

This is Christ coming before God out of the flocks, a ram, a male sheep who became our Sacrificial Lamb offered for our sins. How wonderful! Notice, this verse says that if you *sin through ignorance*—meaning you didn't know any better—then the Lord seeks to guide you back to the holy things of God. That's the reason we need the leadership of the Holy Spirit. The Psalmist said, "He leadeth me beside still waters."

In the Old Testament the scapegoat is a type of Jesus: **And Aaron shall cast lots upon the two goats; one lot for the LORD, and the other lot for the scapegoat. And Aaron shall bring the goat upon which the LORD'S lot fell, and offer him for a sin offering. But the goat, on which the lot fell to be the scapegoat, shall be presented alive before the LORD, to make an atonement with him, and to let him go for a scapegoat into the wilderness** (Leviticus 16:8–10). Jesus became our scapegoat. When we were born again, our sins were put on Him and He carried them away. Study the scapegoat, the way the priest used that scapegoat and sent him away.

GOD'S SHEEP CAN BE CHANGED INTO SINFUL GOATS

Is it carrying a figure of speech too far to say a sheep can be changed into a goat? It's just as easy to change a sheep into a goat when one sins as it is to change a goat into a sheep when one receives salvation. Why would people believe a goat could be changed into a sheep, but say it's impossible for a sheep to be changed into a goat? Oh, consistency, thou art a jewel!

People who insist on having their own way won't accept consistency. Remember, if the devil's goats can become God's sheep, then it's certainly possible for God's sheep to become the devil's goats.

STATEMENT NUMBER THREE:
A CHILD OF GOD CAN NEVER BE LOST

Once a child always a child, proclaim those in unconditional eternal security. Well, let's see what the Bible has to say about it. Although no scripture teaches that once you're saved you cannot be lost, those who believe in unconditional eternal security tell us this is implied in the fact that we become God's children when we are saved; and, no matter how bad a child may become, it is always its father's child. Anyone, however, who has any knowledge about the laws of our land today knows that a father can disinherit a child. The Lord told the man of God that He would disinherit the Israelites; they would no longer be sons and daughters of His. **I will smite them with the pestilence** [diseases]**, and disinherit them** (Numbers 14:12). God help us!

It is a preposterous twist of the Scriptures to claim that those who were once God's children must remain His children no matter how great a sinner they each become. If the Lord reasoned like man, He would turn us over to the devil again as his legitimate property. But just because we were once children of the devil does not mean that we must remain his children, thank God. Neither does it follow that because we were once children of God we will always remain His children. Born-again Christians can backslide if they commit willful sin.

If we say that we have not sinned, we make him a liar, and his word is not in us (I John 1:10). John makes this statement because we were born sinners and must have a Savior.

They answered and said unto him [Jesus]**, Abraham is our father. Jesus saith unto them, If ye were Abraham's children, ye would do the works of Abraham. But now ye seek to kill me, a man that hath told you the truth, which I have heard of God: this did not Abraham** (John 8:39, 40). Jesus didn't let these people get by with claiming

Abraham to be their father. He denied that they were true children of Abraham; they were not doing the works of Abraham. If we are God's children, we do the works of God, not the devil. But the people who claim to be children of God—and continue to sin—are doing the works of the devil. It's impossible to be a child of God if you sin.

THE WORD WAS SPEAKING

Jesus said unto them, If God were your Father, ye would love me: for I proceeded forth and came from God; neither came I of myself, but he sent me. Why do ye not understand my speech? even because ye cannot hear my word (John 8:42,43). The Word was made flesh; the Word was speaking. This is powerful! Some people think I preach strong, but Jesus really went beyond!

Jesus told His accusers just who their father was: **Ye are of your father the devil, and the lusts of your father ye will do. He was a murderer from the beginning, and abode not in the truth, because there is no truth in him. When he speaketh a lie, he speaketh of his own: for he is a liar, and the father of it** (John 8:44). Your father is the one you're going to act like.

The devil was a liar from the beginning; and, if you commit sin, the devil is your father. Think of the people who are in hell today who believed they were going to heaven. So many of them died thinking that everybody sins. Everybody has sinned, but not everybody is sinning; many have been born new.

The Bible tells us to be holy. **Follow peace with all men, and holiness, without which no man shall see the Lord** (Hebrews 12:14). Sin is not included in holiness. Without holiness we will never see the Lord, never see His face. Jesus said, **He that hath seen me hath seen the Father** (John 14:9). When people looked into the face of Jesus, they looked into the face of God. No man since Eden had looked into the face of God until the first person looked into the face of the Babe of Bethlehem.

And because I tell you the truth, ye believe me not. Which of you convinceth me of sin? And if I say the truth, why do ye not believe me? He that is of God heareth God's words: ye therefore hear them not, because ye are not of God (John 8: 45–47). When you have one sin in your heart, your soul is dead. If you are born again and then go back into sin, you are no longer a child of God. Unless you get your soul resurrected into the newness of life, quickened by the Holy Spirit, you'll never get into heaven. A dead soul cannot enter heaven. **The soul that sinneth, it shall die** (Ezekiel 18:20).

SINNERS BELONG TO THE DEVIL

He that committeth sin is of the devil; for the devil sinneth from the beginning. For this purpose the Son of God was manifested, that he might destroy the works of the devil (I John 3:8). Everyone who commits willful sin belongs to the devil. The Son of God was sent to earth where people could see Him, where they could talk to Him and He could talk to them. He came for one purpose: to destroy the works of the devil.

Acts gives an account of a follower of Jesus who fell into the hands of the devil and went to hell: **Judas, which was guide to them that took Jesus. For he was numbered with us** [the disciples], **and had obtained part of this ministry. Now this man purchased a field with the reward of iniquity; and falling headlong, he burst asunder in the midst, and all his bowels gushed out. And it was known unto all the dwellers at Jerusalem; insomuch as that field is called in their proper tongue, Aceldama, that is to say, The field of blood. For it is written in the book of Psalms, Let his habitation be desolate, and let no man dwell therein: and his bishoprick let another take** (Acts 1:16–20).

It's tragic for a person to die lost and go to hell, especially one who was once so close to God that he was numbered with the disciples of Jesus.

Judas had a part in the ministry of Jesus; keep that in mind. **Then he** [Jesus] **called his twelve disciples together, and gave them power and authority over all devils, and to cure diseases** (Luke 9:1). Judas was included in the twelve who were given power over devils. The Word is what counts—the Word, the Word, the Word.

Judas by transgression fell, that he might go to his own place (Acts 1:25). The disciples were choosing a man to take Judas' place. Peter had already said that Judas was numbered with them; in other words, he was like them, a part of them, and had the same power and the same ministry. Nevertheless, Judas fell by transgression that he might go to his own place. Each person chooses his own place: either heaven or hell. Devil possession made Judas go mad, and he committed suicide by hanging himself.

It's incredible that Judas, who once had so much power, fell by transgression! You have to be standing on something in order to fall. What did Judas fall from?—Grace. He backslid. Because he blasphemed against the Holy Ghost, he never could have gotten right with God. Willfully he sinned against God. Some people say that Judas was the devil. No, he was not the devil, but he became devil-possessed. Jesus didn't choose the devil to be one of the twelve.

PETER WAS REBUKED

Jesus rebuked Peter one time as though He was talking to the devil. Why?—Because the devil was talking through Peter. Jesus had been telling the disciples that He was going to die, **that the Son of man must suffer many things, and be rejected of the elders, and of the chief priests, and scribes, and be killed, and after three days rise again. And he spake that saying openly. And Peter took him, and began to rebuke him. But when he had turned about and looked on his disciples, he rebuked Peter, saying, Get thee behind me, Satan: for thou savourest not the things that be of God, but the things that be of men** (Mark 8:31–33). Satan used Peter to try to defeat the Word, and Simon Peter didn't like it when Jesus came against him to rebuke Satan.

POWER TO TRAMPLE THE DEVIL UNDERFOOT

In Matthew's Gospel, Jesus lets us know that one devil can't cast out another devil. **Every kingdom divided against itself is brought to desolation; and every city or house divided against itself shall not stand: And if Satan cast out Satan, he is divided against himself; how shall then his kingdom stand** (Matthew 12:25,26)? This is Jesus' response to the Pharisees who said Jesus cast out devils by the spirit of the devil.

After these things the Lord appointed other seventy also, and sent them two and two before his face into every city and place, whither he himself would come. And the seventy returned again with joy, saying, Lord, even the devils are subject unto us through thy name (Luke 10:1,17). If the seventy had been of the devil they couldn't have cast out devils.

And he [Jesus] **said unto them, I beheld Satan as lightning fall from heaven** (Luke 10:18). Jesus was telling of His greatness, letting His followers know that He was more than just a man. He saw Satan fall; He saw the power of God cast him out of heaven.

THE BOOK OF LIFE

Notwithstanding in this rejoice not, that the spirits are subject unto you; but rather rejoice, because your names are written in heaven (Luke 10:20). Jesus said their names were written in heaven; their names could only have been written in heaven if they were sin-free. The same blood that gives you newness of life and takes you out of the deadness of sin and transgressions is the blood that writes the born-again Christians' names in the Book of Life.

Jesus said, **He that endureth to the end shall be saved** (Matthew 10:22). Jesus' words kill the whole argument of those who believe in unconditional eternal security. First you become saved and come into the grace of God; then you must endure in grace. **For by grace are ye saved through faith; and that not of yourselves: it is the gift of God: Not of works, lest any man should boast** (Ephesians 2:8,9). By grace you are saved, by grace you are lifted out of sin, by grace you live and have your being. You are to live from grace to grace and glorify the Lord in everything, heart, mind, and body. If you leave grace, the only place you can go is disgrace; and disgrace leads to hell.

Sin means death. Isn't that what the Lord told the first man and woman in Eden? People teaching the false doctrine of unconditional eternal security are disputing God; actually, they are calling God a liar. If you don't have that message in your spirit of staying out of sin—and you are sinning—you're not going to make it to heaven. Keep that message before you; it's the voice of God. Sin is absolutely a death sentence. God shows you throughout the Bible how much He hates sin, but also how much He loves sinners and how He tries to change them.

God is true; He is truth and He doesn't lie. If people say something contrary to the Word of God, if they twist one tiny particle of Scripture, then consider them to be liars and deceivers. Look at them as you would look at the devil because the truth is not in them.

STATEMENT NUMBER FOUR:
NO ONE CAN BE UNBORN

Believers in unconditional eternal security come forth with this ridiculous question: If we're born again, how can we be unborn?

Can we be unborn? It's just as easy to be unborn as it is to be born of God; it is simply a reversal of the process. The teaching that those who are born of God cannot be unborn is founded on a misconception of what the new birth really is. I ask people in the healing line if they're born again. Some don't know, and others say they hope so. But many say yes when they don't have the faintest notion of what I'm asking them. They think being born again is a physical change with which people have little or nothing to do. They don't realize it is a spiritual and moral change in a person.

Verily, verily, I say unto you, If a man keep my saying, he shall never see death (John 8:51). Jesus is talking about spiritual death, meaning that people will have eternal life if they keep the sayings of the Lord and live according to the teachings of the Gospel of Jesus Christ.

In a letter to the Romans, Paul warns: **For if ye live after the flesh, ye shall die** (Romans 8:13). **For as many as are led by the Spirit of God, they are the sons** [or daughters] **of God** (Romans 8:14). Backsliders are not led by the Spirit of God, but rather by their own spirit, the spirit of the devil, or the two spirits mixed together.

Nicodemus didn't know Jesus; he probably sought Him out by night because he didn't want anyone to know that he, such a great teacher, was asking questions of a man who was scorned by many. When Jesus told Nicodemus, **Except a man be born again, he cannot see the kingdom of God** (John 3:3), Nicodemus wanted to know: **How can a man be born when he is old? can he enter the second time into his mother's womb, and be born** (John 3:4)?

All people in this doctrine of unconditional eternal security declare that since they once were born again, they are still saved regardless of the fact that they may be drug addicts, fornicators, blasphemers, liars and users of God's name in vain. According to them, they cannot be lost because they were once saved and a saved person can never be lost. They think once saved always saved is unconditional, but it is not.

If you walked after the Spirit, but then started walking after the flesh again, you became the same old sinner you used to be. In fact, the Lord said the latter state of the backslider would be worse than before he or she was saved. Why? The devils that were cast out when the person received salvation picked up reinforcements because they realized they were too weak to hold the fort of that soul alone. **When the unclean spirit is gone out of a man, he walketh through dry places, seeking rest, and findeth none. Then he saith, I will return into my house from whence I came out; and when he is come, he findeth it empty, swept, and garnished. Then goeth he, and taketh with himself seven other spirits more wicked than himself, and they enter in and dwell there: and the last state of that man is worse than the first. Even so shall it be also unto this wicked generation** (Matthew 12:43–45).

THE MOST FRAGILE GIFT

The devil is organized; I've studied him through the Holy Spirit's gift of discerning. You may think you would like to know and see everything about the devil, but you don't really want the gift of discerning. When the Lord gave me the gift of discerning, He told me it was the most fragile of all of the gifts.

A person has to be very particular with this gift, careful to be in touch with God in order to know the spirits—who they are, what they are, what they look like, and if necessary, how many there are. The gift of discerning gives knowledge concerning the subject of devils and demons.

On the other hand, I enjoyed learning about angels—what they look like, what they do, how they work in my services and how I am to work with them. It's easy for me to work with angels, easier than working with people. I never have to battle doubts, fears and misgivings with angels because they're not contaminated with one particle that is unlike God.

How wonderful it is for an angel to talk to you! Usually the angel speaks in the first person; he speaks the exact thoughts of God and nothing of himself. To look into his beautiful face is very different from looking into the faces of devils and demons that are as ugly as God could make them.

BEWARE OF AN ANGEL OF LIGHT

The devil appears as an angel of light, and that's the reason so many people have gotten mixed up and thought an angel came to them to give them a message. It was an angel all right, but it was one of the devil's angels.

The gift of discerning uncovers all demonic spirits.

From a distance, the light they carry looks the same, but it's not the same. When it gets close, the Lord unveils the demon that is hiding behind that light. Be very, very careful.

The Apostle Paul uncovered the devil in a great way. He said, **For Satan himself is transformed into an angel of light** (II Corinthians 11:14). In other words, the devil sends angels with a false gospel to give to people; evil angels are going forth with great destruction today. But thank God, we have the true angels of light through whom the Lord is doing great and wonderful things, mighty manifestations.

STATEMENT NUMBER FIVE:
ETERNAL LIFE CAN'T BE LOST

Just because a life is eternal does not mean that the believer's possession of it is eternal; it's conditional. I say again, when you receive Jesus you receive eternal life; and, as long as you live for Him, you keep that eternal life. But when you fail to live for Jesus, you no longer have that eternal life; now eternal death is in you.

Scientists say that matter is indestructible and must always exist in some form or another. So if I have a pocketknife in my hand, I hold eternal matter that will always exist in some form. However, if I lost my knife, I no longer would have eternal matter in my hand. Were I to find my knife later and pick it up, I would again have eternal matter in my hand. So it is with salvation; if you backslide, you lose it. Salvation is no longer in your soul. Only if you repent of your sins and come back to the Lord can salvation be yours again. Just as I lost the knife, a person may have eternal life and lose it; and, just because life itself is eternal, it does not mean that we have eternal possession of it. That's the reason we must be so careful how we live.

I am afraid of you, lest I have bestowed upon you labour in vain (Galatians 4:11). Paul is writing to the Galatians, some of whom had backslidden. If this letter was not to the backslidden, I don't know who else the letter would have been sent to.

If any man among you seem to be religious, and bridleth not his tongue, but deceiveth his own heart, this man's religion is vain (James 1:26). People who don't bridle their tongues after they receive salvation will find that their glorious salvation has been replaced by spiritual death in their souls. Their religion is vain—no heaven for them unless they repent.

There is no Bible basis for unconditional eternal life in heaven. The scriptures promise everlasting life to only those without sin who *believeth*. Every

English word that ends in *eth* means a continuous work, so *believeth* means to continue to believe. We have a faith, according to scripture, that is a continuous faith; it has to keep going on without the interruption of sin.

For God so loved the world, that he gave his only begotten Son, that whosoever believeth in him should not perish, but have everlasting life (John 3:16). Eternal life is promised to whosoever *believeth*.

Notice again in John 5:24 the word *believeth*. **Verily, verily, I say unto you, He that heareth my word, and believeth on him that sent me, hath everlasting life, and shall not come into condemnation; but is passed from death unto life.** When we receive Jesus, we pass from death to life. Because we were dead in trespasses and sins, we had to have a resurrection. Jesus made it possible for our souls to be resurrected from the dead, and He also made it possible for our bodies to be resurrected come Resurrection Morn.

But without faith it is impossible to please him; for he that cometh to God must believe that he is, and that he is a rewarder of them that diligently seek him (Hebrews 11:6). How can you go to heaven not pleasing God? People who are not pleasing God need a Savior; that's the reason Jesus came.

Ye did run well [you did live for God]**; who did hinder you that ye should not obey the truth** (Galatians 5:7)? It's the truth that sets you free, but you have to keep the truth to stay free. Paul told the Galatians, *You did run well, but not anymore.*

O Foolish Galatians, who hath bewitched you (Galatians 3:1)? Who put this devilish spell on you? The Lord doesn't bewitch anyone, but Paul said these people had been bewitched, taken over by the spirit of the devil. It's dangerous to disobey truth.

I marvel that ye are so soon removed from him that called you into the grace of Christ unto another gospel (Galatians 1:6). This is more of Paul's writing to those foolish Galatians. He was astonished that they had backslidden so soon from the powerful, blood Gospel of Jesus Christ! **There be some that trouble you, and would pervert the gospel of Christ. But though we, or an angel from heaven, preach any other gospel unto you than that which we have preached unto you, let him be accursed** (Galatians 1:7,8). Paul gave them the truth. How sad that the Galatians had gone away from the great teachings he had given them!

If ye continue in the faith grounded and settled, and be not moved away from the hope of the gospel, which ye have heard, and which

was preached to every creature which is under heaven; whereof I Paul am made a minister (Colossians 1:23). Notice: *If you continue in the faith; if you don't backslide . . .* This means you can backslide, for if you don't continue in something, you give it up.

Because the foolish Galatians had given up, Paul was writing to let them know he had told them truth, that he was a minister of truth, and that their lives had to match the truth of God. If your life doesn't match the Gospel, you're not going to heaven.

Therefore if any man [or woman] **be in Christ, he** [or she] **is a new creature** (II Corinthians 5:17). The instant people turn from following their own desires to walking after the Holy Spirit, they become new creatures. To continue to be a new creation, a person must stay in Christ. **There is therefore now no condemnation to them which are in Christ Jesus, who walk not after the flesh, but after the Spirit** (Romans 8:1).

THE LIE THAT WRECKED THE WORLD

The statement that believers can sin and not die is the lie that wrecked the world in the first place. It's the same lie the devil told man when he was living in perfection . . . yet people say they can't backslide.

The Lord has taught us not to listen to the devil

but to listen to what the Holy Spirit is telling us; the Holy Spirit is the author of the whole Word of God. **For the prophecy came not in old time by the will of man: but holy men of God spake as they were moved by the Holy Ghost** (II Peter 1:21).

The lie invented by the devil will keep being told until God is ready to say, *It's enough!* God has let us know through His Word of truth that one day all sin is going to be destroyed.

Whosoever hateth his brother is a murderer: and ye know that no murderer hath eternal life abiding in him (I John 3:15). This verse is talking about your brothers and sisters in the Lord. Only Christians are called brethren; and, if one Christian hates another Christian, eternal life will not abide in that one with the hatred. If you hate your brother in Christ, you're the same as a murderer. No unrepentant murderer has eternal life abiding in him.

For if we sin wilfully [commit a sin knowing it is a sin and don't care] **after that we have received the knowledge of the truth, there remaineth no more sacrifice for sins, But a certain fearful looking for of judgment and fiery indignation, which shall devour the adversaries** (Hebrews 10:26,27). The Lord is our sacrificial offering. If we do not receive Him, then we have no way to heaven.

He that despised Moses' law died without mercy

under two or three witnesses: **Of how much sorer punishment, suppose ye, shall he be thought worthy, who hath trodden under foot the Son of God, and hath counted the blood of the covenant, wherewith he was sanctified, an unholy thing, and hath done despite unto the Spirit of grace** (Hebrews 10:28,29)? This is what God has to say about a backslider; yet people, so-called Christians, are believing the devil when he says once saved always saved—even if the person sins. Millions are involved in this rotten doctrine.

For we know him that hath said, Vengeance belongeth unto me, I will recompense, saith the Lord. And again, The Lord shall judge his people. It is a fearful thing to fall into the hands of the living God (Hebrews 10:30,31). Why would it be fearful to fall into the hands of the living God if you are saved? If you're saved, it isn't fearful and you don't fall into His hands; you live under the protection of His hands.

God is never angry as long as you're right, God right. Why would you be angry with your child if that one were perfectly obedient to everything you told them to do? But if you sin willfully, you have no claim to eternal life unless you can get back to the Lord.

Peter backslid; he cursed, denied the Lord and

said he didn't know Him. **Now Peter sat without in the palace: and a damsel came unto him, saying, Thou also wast with Jesus of Galilee. But he denied before them all, saying, I know not what thou sayest. And after a while came unto him they that stood by, and said to Peter, Surely thou also art one of them; for thy speech bewrayeth thee. Then began he to curse and to swear, saying, I know not the man** (Matthew 26:69,70,73,74).

Do you think Peter had eternal life still abiding in him? No, it took Calvary's blood to deliver him, the blood of Jesus to set him free and heal him from that backslidden condition.

King David backslid. Read his cry to God: **Have mercy upon me, O LORD, for I am in trouble: mine eye is consumed with grief, yea, my soul and my belly. For my life is spent with grief, and my years with sighing: my strength faileth because of mine iniquity, and my bones are consumed** (Psalm 31:9,10).

David was afraid God was never going to take him back. **For I said in my haste, I am cut off from before thine eyes: nevertheless thou heardest the voice of my supplications when I cried unto thee** (Psalm 31:22).

Samson was marked by God in his mother's womb and consecrated unto Him. Look at the power he had for nothing but greatness; yet Samson backslid from God, lost His power, and became a slave to the devil. No one can have eternal life and still be a slave to the devil. It's impossible, and it won't work.

But every man is tempted, when he is drawn away of his own lust, and enticed. Then when lust hath conceived [you've given over to it, put it into practice]**, it bringeth forth sin: and sin, when it is finished, bringeth forth death** (James 1:14,15). This verse is talking about children of God, men and women born of the Spirit of God. Does this sound as though eternal life is unconditional, that you can commit whoredom or other things of the world that the flesh lusts after, things that God said thou shall not partake of and still have eternal life?

Once saved always saved . . . the only way I believe once in grace always in grace is to get in grace and stay there; never backslide. The Bible teaches us to abide in the grace of God.

God places watchmen to warn the sinners. He said if the watchman does not warn the wicked, that the sinner will surely die; then the watchman will be responsible for the blood of those whom he failed to warn. **Son of man, I have made thee a watchman unto the house of Israel: therefore hear the word at my mouth, and give them warning from me. When I say unto the wicked, Thou shalt surely**

die; and thou givest him not warning, nor speakest to warn the wicked from his wicked way, to save his life; the same wicked man shall die in his iniquity; but his blood will I require at thine hand. Yet if thou warn the wicked, and he turn not from his wickedness, nor from his wicked way, he shall die in his iniquity; but thou hast delivered thy soul (Ezekiel 3:17–19).

I give the same warning God is giving to ministers who are preaching that people can sin and not go to hell: The blood of lost people will be on your hands. God told Ezekiel more times than one that if he didn't preach salvation and the people died lost, their blood would be on his hands. Ezekiel earnestly preached God's Word to the people.

STATEMENT NUMBER SIX:
NO CONDEMNATION

Those who believe in this false doctrine stress the first part of Romans 8:1: **There is therefore now no condemnation to them which are in Christ Jesus.** False doctrine states that once you are in Christ Jesus you can never be condemned by heaven, hell, or people; you're an untouchable. What is the truth? The rest of the verse tells us: **who walk not after the flesh, but after the Spirit.** Therefore, if we live after the flesh we shall die. Does that sound like unconditional eternal security?—Absolutely not! Note: These people are in Christ Jesus; they have not sinned and that's why they have no condemnation. The blood applied to your soul is the only thing that makes you an untouchable when it comes to sin, and you have to keep the blood.

Life is in the blood. Spiritually speaking, the soul with divine blood is alive; but, when divine blood is not there, it's dead. People who believe they can never be lost are careful not to read all the scripture! Remember, the Bible says, **Walk in the Spirit, and ye shall not fulfil the lust of the flesh** (Galatians 5: 16). The only way to not give over to the lust of the flesh is to walk and live in the Spirit. According to the Word of God, if you walk after the flesh you are a child of the devil; but, if you walk after the Spirit, you're a child of God.

STATEMENT NUMBER SEVEN: NO SEPARATION

Those who preach once in grace always in grace sometimes quote the latter part of the eighth chapter of Romans. They want to show that nothing can separate them from Christ: **For I am persuaded, that neither death, nor life, nor angels, nor principalities, nor powers, nor things present, nor things to come, Nor height, nor depth, nor** any other creature, shall be able to separate us from the love of God, which is in Christ Jesus our Lord** (Romans 8:38,39). Where is that love? It's in Christ. No external power can separate us from the Lord; remember however, we can separate ourselves through sin. Isaiah the prophet wrote, **But your iniquities have separated between you and your God, and your sins have hid his face from you, that he will not hear** (Isaiah 59:2). Righteousness never hides God's face from you; but sin does, and God won't hear your prayers.

If you're a sinner, your iniquities have separated you from God, eternal life, and the eternal blood—from love, peace, joy, humility, forgiveness of God, and more. You've separated yourself from everything good, from the holiness and righteousness of God.

Jesus conquered death, hell, and the grave to make it possible that we could have an eternal body. Our bodies in heaven will be glorified clay, I'm sure. If you have eternal life, you are a true child of God. But if you sin one willful sin and don't repent, then that eternal life is gone from your soul, and you carry it no longer. You have eternal death.

If we say that we have fellowship with him, and walk in darkness, we lie, and do not the truth (I John 1:6). How can you have fellowship with the

Lord and walk in darkness? Just as quickly as you were born of the Spirit of God, you can lose your salvation. To turn from the light back into darkness, you're lost as far as God is concerned; you're back in the darkness of sin.

Without holiness no man shall see the Lord. We who have eternal life are going to be able to see the Lord as the endless ages roll, not for just a trillion years but on and on.

Jesus said, **For this people's heart is waxed gross, and their ears are dull of hearing, and their eyes they have closed; lest at any time they should see with their eyes, and hear with their ears, and should understand with their heart, and should be converted, and I should heal them** (Matthew 13:15). People are deaf to God's Word because they want to be deaf, blind because they don't want to see. Jesus is also describing people on planet Earth today. The pitiful part is that so many of these people are church members without any God in them; yet, they claim to have eternal life because false doctrine has been preached strongly to them.

The Bible proves that a once-saved woman or man can die lost. It makes it very plain that light and darkness will not mix. **Be ye not unequally yoked together with unbelievers: for what fellowship hath righteousness with unrighteousness?**

and what communion hath light with darkness (II Corinthians 6:14)?

The people which sat in darkness saw great light; and to them which sat in the region and shadow of death light is sprung up (Matthew 4:16). Those who came to the light received eternal life, but they had to keep that light. When you commit a willful sin, you turn out the light in your soul; but, if you unknowingly do something wrong and then later find out it is wrong, fall down before God and repent right then and there. If you're determined to not do it anymore, you're forgiven.

It's wonderful when people turn on God's light; it's a privilege all have through the Gospel of Jesus Christ.

Neither is there salvation in any other: for there is none other name under heaven given among men, whereby we must be saved (Acts 4:12). Jesus is the authority, the foundation. **For other foundation can no man lay than that is laid, which is Jesus Christ** (I Corinthians 3:11). If you are sinning, you're building on the sand and not on the Rock, Christ Jesus. Only the righteous build on that Rock, and the righteous must seek to get every grain of sand between themselves and God out of the way so they can yield completely to the teaching of the Holy Spirit.

It's so essential for us to stay free from sin that the Lord planned in His great wisdom for us to be baptized with power in His Holy Spirit—the fire of God, the keeping power, the fire Moses saw in the burning bush. Although the fire in the burning bush wasn't destructive and didn't destroy the bush, God has a destructive fire that He will use in judgment. Consider how vital the Holy Ghost is to help everyone keep eternal life. He is our keeper, our helper, our guide.

When you're full of the Holy Ghost, He lives inside to teach you and let you know when you're doing right—as long as you want to know. The Holy Ghost lets you know when you've done something wrong, causes you to feel condemnation so you'll repent. If you ignore that condemnation, you become a backslider.

Can a saved person be lost?—Absolutely! Can a person be unborn when it comes to the spiritual birth?—Absolutely! Can a human being change fathers [from God to the devil]?—Absolutely!

GODLY SORROW

No man can come unto the Lord, Jesus said, unless he's drawn by the Spirit. **No man can come to me, except the Father which hath sent me draw him** (John 6:44). The Holy Spirit plays a great part in our conversion, bringing about the change by persuading men and women to turn to God.

If you want to be regenerated, all you have to do is repent of your sins and accept Jesus. **For godly sorrow worketh repentance to salvation** (II Corinthians 7:10). Godly sorrow is being as sorry for your sins as God is that you committed them; nothing less than that will do.

Many people repent of their sins, but *they don't repent with godly sorrow, and that's the secret of it, saith the Lord.* They make an excuse for sin by saying they're weak, but we were all weak in sin. When we realized we were weak and cried out for salvation, godly sorrow let us know we had to have forgiveness. Through the Holy Spirit who convicted us of all our sins, we came into that knowledge. He let us know we were going straight to hell because sin was in our heart and spirit. So, in great heartfelt sorrow we cried out to God. We found forgiveness when we met God on salvation ground. With such sorrow we found it was easy for the Lord to forgive us. We had been brought into the knowledge of truth, convicted and drawn to the Lord by the Holy Spirit of truth who had let us know we were fit citizens for hell with no right to even think about heaven. Begging for mercy, however, we got it and instantly were regenerated, born again of God.

Some people have not understood this statement in the Bible: **I will take the stony heart out of their flesh, and will give them an heart of flesh** (Ezekiel 11:19). This instant birth is not a change in the organs of the body but a change of the spiritual heart. The Lord takes out the stony spiritual heart and gives you a heart that loves Him with all your might, the kind of heart Adam and Eve were given in the beginning.

When the devil gets the heart, the heart is without God's feelings; it only has human feelings or the devil's feelings. The mission of the Holy Spirit is to keep coming down with the Word, the sledgehammer, until He breaks that stony heart—until He removes it through the blood and gives a new heart. Then, born again, we become sons or daughters of God.

DIVINE BLOOD MAKES THE DIFFERENCE

In Eden, Adam and Eve had divine blood in their veins although their bodies were human. In the fall of man and woman, however, they sold out to the devil; they took in poison and the weakness of the devil: human blood. Death is in human blood; and, because of it, there is always a battle, a fight against sickness and disease from the cradle to the grave. Adam and Eve didn't have any battles until they took that poison into their systems.

When we get our new bodies in heaven, we won't have poison but divine blood in our veins as well as in our souls. Our new body will be geared to live forever, inhabited by a soul that has willingly given up all free choice to follow God the Father, God the Son and God the Holy Ghost.

The second Adam, Jesus, came with all power to make it possible for us to have the same choice that God gave Adam and Eve. Just as Adam and Eve went into bondage by making the wrong choice, the Lord delivers us from sin's bondage by our right choice. He sent the Holy Spirit to deal with us, to show us what could be ours. He convicted us of the sinful way we were treating God by getting our attention and letting us know that, if we died in that condition, we could never get inside God's heaven. A dead, barren soul will never reach heaven. Any soul that enters heaven must have the life of God within, the life that God gave the first souls, the first man and woman. For that to happen, a new door had to be made, a new gate into Eden sealed with the blood of Jesus so neither the devil nor carnal man could get in, a door in the form of the Old Rugged Cross.

Spiritual Eden was out of reach of man and woman for thousands of years. It looked as though there never would be another chance for man and woman to live in that Eden. Somehow Eden would have to be brought back; and at last, the second Adam, Jesus, came. He brought the Gospel, the good news to let people know they can be born new, created in righteousness and holiness—not man's holiness, but true holiness.

Jesus gave His life for you to live in spiritual Eden, for that's the only way it could be done. Many people don't realize the significance of Jesus' divinity. Although He had a human body and a human mind, He had divine blood in His veins. His soul was as holy and pure as the soul the first man received in Eden.

The Bible says, **Put on the new man, which after God is created in righteousness and true holiness** (Ephesians 4:24). To be created in righteousness and holiness means you are a new creature like the man God made in Eden—as far as your soul is concerned. Bury the old person and become a new you. Take on the same personality that the second Adam brought, and realize He didn't come with anything less than the divine personality for all of us.

The instant birth is a real change. A new heart is wrought in you by the Holy Spirit as you cooperate with the will of God one hundred percent. The moment you turn from walking after the flesh and begin to walk after the Spirit you are no longer carnally or worldly minded, but rather you are spiritually minded. You can't have a mind of the world and a mind of the Spirit at the same time.

Although contaminated down through the years, man still desired to have a close relationship with God. He couldn't get into that spiritual Eden, but his thoughts went to it. The prophets, both major and minor, never fully understood salvation; however, the Lord would shine the light upon them at different times, and through the Holy Ghost they would write about the coming of the Messiah, about Jesus Christ. Even Moses prophesied about Jesus' coming: **The LORD thy God will raise up unto thee a Prophet from the midst of thee, of thy brethren, like unto me; unto him ye shall hearken** (Deuteronomy 18:15).

When God at last did raise up a Prophet for all to hear, only some really heard Him; most didn't heed what He had to say. But all who denied Him went to hell; they had nothing whatsoever with which to justify themselves in the eyes of God.

Man longed for something he thought he could never have and would never find. The Old Testament prophets looked forward to the day they would have more light, when they could offer the people all that the Lord was revealing; but they didn't live to see it. However, we're not only here to see it, but also to experience it and to live it. How sad that today many are still in darkness because preachers, teachers, and priests have put them there, led them into the night.

BE NOT OF THE WORLD

Jesus said, **They are not of the world, even as I am not of the world** (John 17:16). Can you say today that you are not of the world? I can say in all truth that I am not of the world. I am in the world; I walk upon the earth, but I take no part in the sins of this world.

Love not the world, neither the things that are in the world. If any man love the world, the love of the Father is not in him (I John 2:15). If you're a part of this world and love the world, you're not a part of the Father. You can't go to heaven without loving God.

The Bible is not talking about the world of good things God has made—the grass, trees, sunshine, moon, stars, vegetables, fish and so forth. It hasn't been these things that have ruined God's world; it's been the world of people and the devil.

Wherefore come out from among them, and be ye separate, saith the Lord, and touch not the unclean thing; and I will receive you (II Corinthians

6:17). In many cases people can't expect to win over the devil because they won't let go of self and give themselves wholly and completely to God. But the Early Church did and they won.

TO BE CARNALLY MINDED IS DEATH

When you no longer have a carnal mind, you don't tell or listen to dirty jokes; you don't indulge in pornography of any kind. You have clean eyes, clean ears, clean speech, and a new heart that beats in rhythm with the heart of God, with His joy, peace and gladness. With the same desires as God, your heart flows with the same blood—divine blood. Use the blood that flows for you.

For to be carnally minded is death (Romans 8:6). Does that sound as though you're going to heaven with a carnal mind? Does that sound like once in grace always in grace? Does that sound like unconditional eternal security? It sounds like conditional eternal security to me. **Wherefore let him that thinketh he standeth take heed lest he fall** (I Corinthians 10:12). We can stand only through the grace of God.

To be carnally minded means you're dead for time and all eternity unless you get a resurrection. All who are carnally minded are spiritually dead; there's no life of God in them. Don't let the world influence you in any way by what it does, what it says, where it goes and what it watches.

Therefore, brethren, we are debtors, not to the flesh, to live after the flesh (Romans 8:12). We're not in debt to the flesh. We don't owe the flesh anything. But have you ever wondered how much you owe heaven since Christ is yours? Everything He brought, everything He taught, the whole Will of the New Testament is yours. He made you a joint-heir with Him, not just an heir to the Kingdom, but a joint-heir to share equally with Him. **And if children, then heirs; heirs of God, and joint-heirs with Christ; if so be that we suffer with him, that we may be also glorified together** (Romans 8:17).

Do you hear the words of God down through these thousands of years? It's the same voice, the same Spirit; but judgment has gone out of it, and the grace that Jesus brought is in that voice today.

But if ye through the Spirit do mortify the deeds of the body, ye shall live (Romans 8:13). Through the Spirit we are keepers of the flesh, responsible for our flesh. We are responsible for our mind, for what we take part in, and for what our bodies do. If you keep the body under control of the Spirit and under the blood, God's grace is sufficient and you shall live. How long?—Forever and ever. No one has ever found the end of eternity; anything eternal doesn't end or it wouldn't be eternal.

WALK IN THE LIGHT

But if we walk in the light, as he is in the light, we have fellowship one with another, and the blood of Jesus Christ his Son cleanseth us from all sin (I John 1:7). Being cleansed from all sin brings you into a spiritual Eden and makes you a fit citizen for heaven. A strait gate has been placed down here by the hand of God, and you have to go through that strait gate called Calvary to start out on the narrow road leading to heaven.

It's wonderful to walk in the light of God! There's no darkness in God, no shadows. When Jesus conquered death He took all the shadows out of the valley of death. The Psalmist said, **Yea, though I walk through the valley of the shadow of death, I will fear no evil: for thou art with me; thy rod and thy staff they comfort me** (Psalm 23:4). Children of God see no shadows when they go through the valley of death because Jesus and the Holy Spirit are there to help them cross Jordan.

Oh, how the Lord loves the steps of those that follow the footsteps of Jesus: holy, human steps! But if you cease to walk in the blood light, the blood cannot cleanse you, and you are no longer a child of God. Just as God threw man and woman out of Eden, He will throw all out of His Kingdom who no longer belong.

BE YE PERFECT

It's time for us to look to God, to believe God for His greatness and the reality of it. Jesus said, **Be ye therefore perfect, even as your Father which is in heaven is perfect** (Matthew 5:48). Nothing is perfect about sin. The Lord would never call people perfect with one seed of sin in them, and one tiny seed destroyed the great plan of God. This whole planet would have been paradise for the seed of Adam and Eve had they not failed God, and the devil would have been in the lake of fire thousands of years ago with all the fallen angels and demons, also, but not so.

But as many as received him, to them gave he power to become the sons of God, even to them that believe on his name (John 1:12). Now how could you be a son of God and have a seed of sin? It's impossible; it won't work. No sin can enter heaven; God will not embrace any sin. All sin has to be forgiven outside the gates of Glory. Inside the gates there will be no forgiveness for sin, for there will be no sin for God to forgive. Only those forgiven through the blood of Jesus will be in heaven.

To as many as receive Him, receive the Lord in their hearts, receive the divine blood, He gives power to become sons of God. You have to be in the family of God to live with that family in heaven. People outside the family of God needn't expect to live in heaven for all eternity.

DO YOU BALK?

Failure through weakness or lack of knowledge does not make you a child of the devil. If there is a weakness in your praying, fasting or reading the Word, it doesn't automatically mean you're backslidden; it means you're not drawing on the blood the way you need to. The Bible tells you that you can know the will of God; but, if you're not willing to do the will of God, why should He give you full knowledge of it? Why should He take the trouble to try to guide you daily through His Holy Spirit when you're balking all the way?

Growing up on the farm, we had a team of horses that balked, and they remind me today of a lot of so-called Christians. Those horses were fine when pulling an empty wagon. An empty wagon rattles a lot, but the horses didn't mind that at all. However, when Dad loaded the wagon with wood he had just cut for winter, those horses would throw their front hooves up into the air and refuse to pull; they were not going to move that load. Dad was a gentle man, looked after his animals and kept them well fed; but he would have to get a switch about two or three yards long and give them some real horse discipline. It was the only way he could conquer them, and those horses would finally pull the load—until the next time. Like children they would act good for a while, but then they would forget, balk again and get the same treatment. Dad finally got rid of them.

You may balk at the Lord for a while; but, like my dad with those horses, He will finally get rid of you. A lot of people are like those horses. They want the Lord to feed them, want to be fat in the things of God, but they don't want to help take His Gospel to the world. Many Christians today are sitting on the sidelines not doing anything for God while billions of people are lost and undone without Him. Jesus came to set the captives free, and what a great price heaven paid for our freedom! I don't want to forget His great sacrifice in my work for Him; what about you?

If there is a weakness in you, and you're not in the Bible the way you ought to be, not talking to God as much as you should and not fasting, know that you have help. The Holy Spirit came to be your helper, and He will give you an appetite; He will help you if you let Him, if you decide you want to do the will of God and if you want God's help. But if you deliberately open up to sin, you're walking after the flesh; you're now a child of the devil no matter how close to God you once were.

PLEASANT TO THE EYES

It was so easy for man and woman to go into sin in Eden! **And when the woman saw that the tree was good for food, and that it was pleasant to the eyes, and a tree to be desired to make one wise, she took of the fruit thereof, and did eat, and gave also unto her husband with her; and he did eat** (Genesis 3:6). The forbidden fruit was pleasant to the eyes. Sin is pleasant to the eyes but bitter in the belly.

Something pleasant to the eyes that seems to make one wise has drawn people into the occult, witchcraft, voodooism, and all the other darknesses of the devil. People want to be wise, to know the future; and many seek that ungodly wisdom in spiritualism and the occult today. They go to séances hoping to see their dead or hear the voice of a loved one, but they're in contact with nothing but familiar spirits. Familiar spirits will dress like your loved one and mimic that one's voice until you can't tell the difference.

In this final hour you must learn how seducing

devils work. God hasn't ever allowed as many of them on earth as He is allowing now; it's all-out war. Some Christians can hardly wait to get the newspaper so they can see what the astrologer has to say. Astrologers and what they are telling you are of the devil. Were Daniel here to preach to you, you would drop that astrology column like a hot potato just out of the oven.

Preacher, I only want to see what my day is going to be like.

Well, when you depend on what an astrologer says, your day is going to be like the devil wants it to be. The wicked kings in Babylon were surrounded by astrologers. Astrology was started by the devil, and one day it's going back to hell where it came from.

Isaiah the prophet told the Children of Israel about the destiny of the astrologers: **Thou art wearied in the multitude of thy counsels. Let now the astrologers, the stargazers, the monthly prognosticators, stand up, and save thee from these things that shall come upon thee. Behold, they shall be as stubble; the fire shall burn them; they shall not deliver themselves from the power of the flame: there shall not be a coal to warm at, nor fire to sit before it** (Isaiah 47:13,14). The Children of Israel were looking to astrologers, soothsayers and so forth, but Isaiah let them know the fate of those in the occult. It was straight talk from the voice of God.

Can eternal life be lost? Of course it can. *Every true man and woman of God should know the deceit of this rotten, damnable doctrine of unconditional eternal security, saith the Lord.* Not only has it ushered untold multitudes into hell, the devil is still using it to lead armies of more souls right toward the pits of damnation. You are going to meet this false doctrine again and again. Some of you meet it in your family every time you come together for a holiday celebration. You can meet this doctrine at almost any funeral. How sad indeed!

GO AND SIN NO MORE

And the times of this ignorance God winked at; but now commandeth all men everywhere to repent (Acts 17:30). What does that mean? God is calling everyone out of sin, calling everyone into righteousness, into holiness, into the new birth. Why be born again and made completely new, as Jesus told Nicodemus, and then say you can't live free from sin? If the brand-new person cannot live free from sin, there would be no need for Jesus to make that one brand-new, would there? And there would be no need for us to receive a born-again experience if we were going to continue to travel paths of sin.

This is the big question for people who believe they can't live free from sin: ***How many sins can you commit and still go to heaven?*** We'd have to know where to stop, wouldn't we? So there has to be a number. The Lord has all wisdom and knowledge, and He wouldn't leave us in the night; He would number how many sins each one is allowed. But the Bible says that God can't look upon sin. **Thou art of purer eyes than to behold evil, and canst not look on iniquity** (Habakkuk 1:13). That means God will not embrace any kind of sin.

Lucifer was cast out of heaven because of false pride. He was lifted up and that heart of his yielded to ego. He thought he could ascend above the throne of God; it's in the Word of God. **Thine heart was lifted up because of thy beauty, thou hast corrupted thy wisdom by reason of thy brightness** (Ezekiel 28:17).

JESUS CAME TO RESCUE US FROM SIN

Preachers who preach that everybody sins are themselves sinning. God gives me revelations about different ones, and I let them know about their sins. Some of them won't come out of their sins; they're still going to do what they want to do. They will be in hell for it, too.

Jesus came not to condemn the world, but to forgive. **For God sent not his Son into the world to condemn the world; but that the world through him might be saved** (John 3:17). The world was already condemned under the penalty of death; death was upon all men and women. The Bible tells us death reigned for thousands of years. Jesus came to rescue us from that penalty of death; but that penalty of death is not ours unless there is some sin in our hearts and in our lives. One speck of sin won't get through the gate of Glory. With one speck of sin in your heart, the Lord won't be looking upon you in heaven because He cannot look upon sin. He will not embrace it, will not endorse it—and you won't be there.

A PERFECT HEART

Jesus made it possible for you to have a perfect heart that desires the will of God all the time. Beating in harmony with God, that heart takes on the mind of Jesus, knows the thoughts of God and delights in them. There is no static; the devil can't keep the prayers of that heart from being answered.

It was the perfect voice of the heart of Jesus that walked upon the earth and talked faith to a man who had just received word that his little daughter was dead and there was no need to trouble the Master any longer. **As soon as Jesus heard the word that was spoken, he saith unto the ruler of the synagogue, Be not afraid, only believe** (Mark 5:36). The person who said not to trouble the Master any longer didn't know life was walking down the road toward the home of Jairus.

And he [Jesus] **cometh to the house of the ruler of the synagogue, and seeth the tumult, and them that wept and wailed greatly. And when he was come in, he saith unto them, Why make ye this ado, and weep? the damsel is not dead, but sleepeth. And they laughed him to scorn. But when he had put them all out, he taketh the father and the mother of the damsel, and them that were with him, and entereth in where the damsel was lying. And he took the damsel by the hand, and said unto her, Tal-i-tha cu-mi; which is, being interpreted, Damsel, I say unto thee, arise. And straightway the damsel arose, and walked; for she was of the age of twelve years. And they were astonished with a great astonishment** (Mark 5:38–42).

In this final hour the life of the eternal Word of God is going to be walking in us all over the world. We'll pay the price in fastings, prayers, and living in the Word. As living epistles we will believe the whole Word of God, and God will supply our needs—and above—so we can meet His needs. On call, not only eight hours or twelve hours a day, but twenty-four hours around the clock, we will be obedient to Him in prayers, fastings and in every way.

The Lord called me to be on duty for Him in the healing ministry twenty-four hours a day. He could wake me at any hour, and I never objected. I didn't know how long His visits would be, but I treasured every minute no matter the condition of my body. Sometimes the visitations would last for hours. He might let me go to sleep for an hour or so, relaxing me through and through; then He would wake me with His gentle touch, as gently as you would wake a small child, and my mind would be clear. His wonderful Word was so soothing, so uplifting that I felt I was living and dining in Eden. In His presence there is no fog, no doubt; I didn't have one particle of doubt. He was showing me what would happen, and I believed it all; and I still believe it all today!

CHAPTER 2

Letters From The Lord

A LETTER TO EPHESUS

Study in the book of Revelation the letters to the seven churches, letters that Jesus dictated to John the Revelator. To the first of the seven churches, the Church at Ephesus, Jesus said, **I know thy works, and thy labour, and thy patience, and how thou canst not bear them which are evil: and thou hast tried them which say they are apostles, and are not, and hast found them liars: And hast borne, and hast patience, and for my name's sake hast laboured, and hast not fainted. Nevertheless I have somewhat against thee, because thou hast left thy first love** (Revelation 2:2–4). The Church at Ephesus was doing many good things, but God wasn't first in their lives any longer. They had left Him and were turning to the world.

Remember therefore from whence thou art fallen (Revelation 2:5). The Church at Ephesus had fallen from the great grace of first love. Without love, the Bible tells us, we are nothing. **Though I have all faith, so that I could remove mountains, and have not charity** [love]**, I am nothing** (I Corinthians 13:2).

You can't get into heaven without love, and you can't go to heaven being critical, bitter and gossipy; you need a love-tongue to enter God's heaven, to sing God's praises and to rejoice in the Lord. The Lord wants you to praise Him, to be glad; but, when poison defiles your tongue, He doesn't hear you. He turns you off, becomes deaf to your voice.

God is no longer wasting His time listening to the spew of the devil, that snake-talk coming forth from the ungodly; however, their words are all recorded. Those words will be there to convict the sinner. Revelation 2:5, **Repent, and do the first works; or else I will come unto thee quickly, and will remove thy candlestick out of his place, except thou repent.** The Ephesian Church, one of the candlesticks, was going into a backslidden state; and only repentance would save them.

Some people think joining a church will take them

to heaven. I asked a woman in one of my revivals, "Are you saved?"

"I belong to a church," she replied.

"Your church won't save you."

She looked at me with arrogance, "I believe mine will," she said. The church she belonged to believed once in grace always in grace. I don't know whether she ever made it to heaven or not, but she believed her church would take her there. I left her. The Bible doesn't teach that a church will take you to heaven; it's the blood that will take you there.

One missionary on her deathbed left this testimony: "I have done many works for the Lord, but I'm not going to heaven through my works. I'm going through the blood of Jesus." Isn't that wonderful! I've never forgotten her dying statement, and it was years ago when I read about it. *I'm going to heaven through the blood of Jesus!* Her last words were about the blood.

Jesus purchased the Church with His own blood, and He has the right to say who will go into heaven and who won't. Jesus is the door, remember, and you have to go through the door, the Word, to get into heaven.

TO THE CHURCH IN SMYRNA

To the church in Smyrna Jesus said: **These things saith the first and the last, which was dead, and is alive; I know thy works, and tribulation, and poverty, (but thou art rich) and I know the blasphemy of them which say they are Jews, and are not, but are the synagogue of Satan** (Revelation 2:8,9). Jesus was telling this church that He knew the things they had been through, and then He went on to say, **Fear none of those things which thou shalt suffer: behold, the devil shall cast some of you into prison, that ye may be tried; and ye shall have tribulation ten days: be thou faithful unto death, and I will give thee a crown of life** (Revelation 2:10). The crown of life is eternal life. Jesus told this church that they were doing a good job, and that they had to be faithful unto death.

Read what the Lord said to the different churches every once in a while, and apply it to your own life; see where you stand.

Be thou faithful unto death, and I will give thee a crown of life. Faithful how long?—Unto death.

THE PERGAMOS CHURCH

And to the angel of the church in Pergamos write; These things saith he which hath the sharp sword with two edges; I know thy works

and where thou dwellest, even where Satan's seat is: and thou holdest fast my name, and hast not denied my faith, even in those days wherein Antipas was my faithful martyr, who was slain among you, where Satan dwelleth. But I have a few things against thee, because thou hast there them that hold the doctrine of Balaam, who taught Balac to cast a stumblingblock before the children of Israel, to eat things sacrificed unto idols, and to commit fornication. So hast thou also them that hold the doctrine of the Nicolaitans, which thing I hate. Repent; or else I will come unto thee quickly, and will fight against them with the sword of my mouth. He that hath an ear, let him hear what the Spirit saith unto the churches; To him that overcometh will I give to eat of the hidden manna, and will give him a white stone, and in the stone a new name written, which no man knoweth saving he that receiveth it** (Revelation 2:12–17). Jesus dictated these things to John, and Jesus said you have to be an overcomer—that means overcoming all sin.

TO THE ANGEL OF THYATIRA

And unto the angel of the church in Thyatira write; These things saith the Son of God, who hath his eyes like unto a flame of fire, and his feet are like fine brass; I know thy works, and charity, and service, and faith, and thy patience, and thy works; and the last to be more than the first. Notwithstanding I have a few things against thee, because thou sufferest that woman Jezebel, which calleth herself a prophetess, to teach and to seduce my servants to commit fornication, and to eat things sacrificed unto idols. And I gave her space to repent of her fornication; and she repented not. Behold, I will cast her into a bed, and them that commit adultery with her into great tribulation, except they repent of their deeds. And I will kill her children with death; and all the churches shall know that I am he which searcheth the reins and hearts: and I will give unto every one of you according to your works (Revelation 2:18–23).

Jesus brought a great accusation against this church, but He went on to say to those who were not involved that He wouldn't put any of this judgment upon them. **But unto you I say, and unto the rest in Thyatira, as many as have not this doctrine, and which have not known the depths of Satan, as they speak; I will put upon you none other burden. But that which ye have already hold fast till I come** (Revelation 2:24,25). We're not responsible for the sins of others, and here Jesus is speaking to the part of this church that still had eternal life.

And he that overcometh, and keepeth my works unto the end, to him will I give power over the nations: And he shall rule them with a rod of iron; as the vessels of a potter shall they be broken to shivers: even as I received of my Father (Revelation 2:26,27).

SARDIS: READY TO DIE

And to the church at Sardis: **These things saith he that hath the seven Spirits of God, and the seven stars; I know thy works, that thou hast a name that thou livest, and art dead. Be watchful, and strengthen the things which remain, that are ready to die: for I have not found thy works perfect before God. Remember therefore how thou hast received and heard, and hold fast, and repent. If therefore thou shalt not watch, I will come on thee as a thief, and thou shalt not know what hour I will come upon thee. Thou hast a few names even in Sardis which have not defiled their garments; and they shall walk with me in white: for they are worthy. He that overcometh, the same shall be clothed in white raiment; and I will not blot out his name out of the book of life** (Revelation 3:1–5). Can your name be blotted out of the Book of Life? This passage lets you know it can be. Jesus says that he who overcomes will be clothed in white raiment, the righteousness of the saints. What has to be overcome?—This old world of sin, all sin. Eternal life is promised to the overcomer, and he that believeth and liveth righteously is an overcomer.

You can't be of Christ if you stop believing in His mission, in the Gospel He brought, and in what the Father had told Him. Had Jesus stopped believing, He would have lost out; the second Adam would have been defeated. But Jesus wasn't defeated.

The Lord lets us know, **For whosoever shall be ashamed of me and of my words, of him shall the Son of man be ashamed, when he shall come in his own glory, and in his Father's, and of the holy angels** (Luke 9:26).

PHILADELPHIA: READY FOR THE RAPTURE

And now to the church of Philadelphia: **Because thou hast kept the word of my patience, I also will keep thee from the hour of temptation, which shall come upon all the world, to try them that dwell upon the earth. Behold, I come quickly: hold that fast which thou hast, that no man take thy crown** (Revelation 3:10,11). Jesus meant that when He comes, it will be quick. You must hold fast the good things so you'll be ready.

Him that overcometh will I make a pillar in the temple of my God, and he shall go no more out: and I will write upon him the name of my God, and the name of the city of my God, which is new Jerusalem, which cometh down out of heaven from my God: and I will write upon him my new name. He that hath an ear, let him hear what the Spirit saith unto the churches (Revelation 3:12,13). If you have kept the word of God's patience, you have eternal life. Either eternal life is in your soul or an eternal living death; there are only two choices.

Does God expect man and woman to live free from all sin? Is it a teaching of the Word? Yes, it is. God wants you to have plenty of scriptures against sin and plenty for holy living.

THE LAODICEANS WERE LUKEWARM

And unto the angel of the church of the Laodiceans write; These things saith the Amen, the faithful and true witness, the beginning of the creation of God; I know thy works, that thou art neither cold nor hot: I would thou wert cold or hot. So then because thou art lukewarm, and neither cold nor hot, I will spue thee out of my mouth (Revelation 3:14–16). Only devout Christians are in the mouth of God; God will spew out lukewarm

Christians. He can't stand lukewarmness.

But with eternal life bubbling in your soul, you're anything but lukewarm. Eternal life gives you an appetite for God and the things of God; it helps you turn your back on the world. Just like the devil tried to entice Eve, he tries to entice you; but, with the Holy Ghost living on the inside, you have the advantage. The lukewarm have no such advantage.

Because thou sayest, I am rich, and increased with goods, and have need of nothing; and knowest not that thou art wretched, and miserable, and poor, and blind, and naked: I counsel thee to buy of me gold tried in the fire, that thou mayest be rich; and white raiment, that thou mayest be clothed, and that the shame of thy nakedness do not appear; and anoint thine eyes with eye-salve [the Word of God], **that thou mayest see** (Revelation 3:17,18). This describes many people today, and again I say, it would be well for you to study all the Lord dictated to John.

THE CHURCH BACKSLID

Can a person backslide? The Church of Jesus Christ backslid. For thirty-three years they had lived in grace, but then they began to fall into disgrace. Later, Emperor Constantine recognized Christianity because man's Christianity had become popular and

Constantine wanted to be in control.

Some of you have never studied Church history; it would be helpful to find out how the Church backslid and went into almost total darkness. The candle of the Gospel was barely flickering. God, however, always had a few who were faithful to Him, and the Gospel candle kept giving forth a wee bit of light.

A great warning is found in Revelation: **For I testify unto every man that heareth the words of the prophecy of this book, If any man shall add unto these things** [and that means all other books of the Bible as well], **God shall add unto him the plagues that are written in this book** [the plague of death is in this Book]: **And if any man shall take away from the words of the book of this prophecy, God shall take away his part out of the book of life, and out of the holy city, and from the things which are written in this book** (Revelation 22: 18,19).

If you take something out of God's Gospel, He will take your name out of the Book of Life. No good promise will be yours if you backslide; there's nothing from God for the unrepentant backslider but judgment, damnation, vengeance, hellfire and brimstone. Eternal damnation is for all who do not live in the righteousness of God.

The only way your name can be written in the

Book of Life is through the divine blood that Jesus brought, and the only thing that can keep your name in that book is your yielding to eternal blood grace. The Book of Life is eternal; but, if your name is in it today, that doesn't mean it will stay there if you sin. It doesn't mean that you have eternal rights to it and can do anything you want to do. You have the privilege of choosing either the blessing of eternal life or the curse of eternal death.

One day an angel of God will shout the words throughout the whole earth: *Time shall be no more!* **And the angel which I saw stand upon the sea and upon the earth lifted up his hand to heaven, And sware by him that liveth for ever and ever, who created heaven, and the things that therein are, and the earth, and the things that therein are, and the sea, and the things which are therein, that there should be time no longer** (Revelation 10:5,6). Now is the beginning of eternity for you: Will yours be eternal death or eternal life, eternal hell and the lake of fire or eternal heaven? The choice, I say again, is yours. The message from God must go forth in this final hour.

A FOUNTAIN HAS BEEN OPENED

As very man, Jesus had divine blood in His veins. Divinity took on the fashion of a man and showed us the importance of obedience: **And being found in fashion as a man, he** [Jesus] **humbled himself, and became obedient unto death, even the death of the cross** (Philippians 2:8). Since Jesus gave His life for our salvation, we have no excuse for sin at all.

Sin is destructive and damnable; but blood-grace edifies and builds up. All good and perfect gifts come through the blood-grace from heaven. **Every good gift and every perfect gift is from above, and cometh down from the Father of lights, with whom is no variableness, neither shadow of turning** (James 1:17).

Sin comes from the devil. When man fell into the hands of the devil, he fell into everything bad: sickness and physical death as well as spiritual death.

Eternal life is wonderful, glorious. Protect and hold fast to the eternal life you received at Calvary; it can be found in no other place. A fountain has opened for us, Calvary's fountain to take away sin and uncleanness. Salvation is ours, purchased by the blood. **For ye are bought with a price: therefore glorify God in your body, and in your spirit, which are God's** (I Corinthians 6:20). Jesus set you free from being a slave of the devil. You're absolutely free from sin, and you must remain free.

When a soul has divine blood, it has no sin. Eternal

life is real and can never be destroyed. But the possession of eternal life in heaven can be destroyed; you can destroy it by sin.

You have no right to sin, to trample the blood of Jesus underfoot, or to disgrace the blood; backsliding is a disgrace to the blood of Jesus Christ. Samson became a disgrace and Peter became a disgrace. Judas became such a disgrace that he was beyond redemption. Think of the repulsive spirit that comes up in you at the mention of Judas' name. Judas sold Jesus, sold the blood.

JESUS BROUGHT A HEALING BALM

Oppression and depression come from the devil, but Jesus brought a healing balm. How sad that some Christians won't use it! The devil gets people's attention and tells them how bad and awful their situation is. But if people would start singing praises and hymns to God, they'd have a glad day after a while. It's been promised and it would come. Why should you be depressed? Get rid of all depression through the blood. Your Father is rich, and you're an heir; eternal life abides in you. Look to Jesus; He's your example and He won; realize that you can be a winner, too. *I'm in your steps, dear Jesus; I'm a winner!*

Just as Jesus was headed for the ascension, we're

headed for the Rapture. It was easy when it came time for Jesus to go up, easy for Him to ascend. After Jesus had risen from the tomb, He told Mary Magdalene not to touch Him. **Jesus saith unto her, Touch me not; for I am not yet ascended to my Father, but go to my brethren, and say unto them, I ascend unto my Father, and your Father; and to my God, and your God** (John 20:17). Later, however, Jesus told His followers to touch Him all they wanted to. **Behold my hands and my feet, that it is I myself: handle me, and see; for a spirit hath not flesh and bones, as ye see me have** (Luke 24:39).

It doesn't take any time to get to heaven. You take a step here on earth, and your next step lands you on Glory's shore. The way the Lord is pouring out His Spirit is one of the great endtime signs of Jesus' soon coming, and the Bride of Christ is being made ready.

Be careful in this final hour. As you read earlier, the book of Revelation contains seven letters dictated to the seven churches by Jesus Christ. This is the only time we have record of Jesus dictating letters, and they are important letters. Something is in every letter to help you wake up. If you are lukewarm and no longer have that first love, face it; know you don't have it and seek God for it again.

Do you believe the Lord hears you every time you pray? Jesus believed the Father heard Him. Jesus said, **Father, I thank thee that thou hast heard me. And I knew that thou hearest me always: but because of the people which stand by I said it, that they may believe that thou hast sent me** (John 11:41,42). Trust the Lord to hear your sincere prayers when you pray in His divine will.

CHAPTER 3

Sin Brings Judgment

Christ knew no sin in His life until He took our sins and sicknesses. **For he hath made him to be sin for us, who knew no sin; that we might be made the righteousness of God in him** (II Corinthians 5:21). But Jesus did not commit sin, and He was never sick. The first Adam was never sick until he fell into sin and the curse came upon him. **Is any sick among you? let him call for the elders of the church; and let them pray over him, anointing him with oil in the name of the Lord: And the prayer of faith shall save the sick, and the Lord shall raise him up; and if he have committed sins, they shall be forgiven him** (James 5:14,15).

We need to study Jesus now more than ever. He

lived here on earth for thirty-three years as very man as well as very God; He was in His place—spiritual Eden.

The Word of God closes with Jesus, the second Adam, and His Bride under the tree of life. **Blessed are they that do his commandments, that they may have right to the tree of life, and may enter in through the gates into the city** (Revelation 22: 14).

Some people want to know what happened to the tree of life. You find out in Revelation: **In the midst of the street of it, and on either side of the river, was there the tree of life, which bare twelve manner of fruits, and yielded her fruit every month: and the leaves of the tree were for the healing of the nations** (Revelation 22:2). The tree of life is in heaven.

Don't you wonder about these things? Don't you hunger and thirst after more knowledge of the truth of righteousness? The Lord gives us little glimpses of heaven here and there. Not many days pass that my mind doesn't go to Eden. I love Eden, love the things in Eden when God had no disappointment in man.

JEALOUSY IS AS CRUEL AS THE GRAVE

Cain, the son of Adam and Eve, was the first to commit murder. **And Cain talked with Abel his brother: and it came to pass, when they were in the field, that Cain rose up against Abel his brother, and slew him** (Genesis 4:8). There wouldn't have been a murder had sin not entered Eden; but today we see that Cain-spirit raging all over the world through jealousy, violence, and killing. Because Abel was righteous, his brother hated him. God accepted Abel, and jealousy took Cain over. Jealousy comes from the devil. **Jealousy is cruel as the grave: the coals thereof are coals of fire, which hath a most vehement flame** (Song of Solomon 8:6).

And the LORD said unto Cain, Why art thou wroth? and why is thy countenance fallen? If thou doest well, shalt thou not be accepted? and if thou doest not well, sin lieth at the door (Genesis 4:6,7). When sin is at your door, the judgment of God is there as well. Righteousness and holiness belong to you only if you don't sin.

Through the light of holy living, Abel saw what sin had done to his parents. He saw the sicknesses, the diseases, how his father through the sweat of his brow had to work to grow his food from the earth. It was never to have been. **And unto Adam he**

[God] said, Because thou hast hearkened unto the voice of thy wife, and hast eaten of the tree, of which I commanded thee, saying, Thou shalt not eat of it: cursed is the ground for thy sake; in sorrow shalt thou eat of it all the days of thy life; Thorns also and thistles shall it bring forth to thee; and thou shalt eat the herb of the field; In the sweat of thy face shalt thou eat bread, till thou return unto the ground; for out of it wast thou taken: for dust thou art, and unto dust shalt thou return (Genesis 3:17–19). Abel observed the results of one sin. He was a good worker, a holy man; and God was proud of him. But Cain took on the spirit of the devil.

The devil in Cain's soul contaminated his whole spirit; the spirit of man was taken over by evil. God never intended that. The envy, strife, and jealousy of Cain turned into murder.

What a cruel thing Abel's murder was! Sin makes God helpless to direct man and his paths. The devil will cause sinners to commit any sin he can get them to commit, and then he'll insist that they blame God. The devil takes over their thinking when deceit is in their heart.

We don't know whether Adam and Eve ever got back to God. The Lord doesn't give us any record of it. We only know that there was no deceit in Abel's heart; he had the Spirit of the living God in him.

In searching Genesis we come across different things that shed light on the people of that time. **And Adam knew his wife again; and she bare a son, and called his name Seth: For God, said she, hath appointed me another seed instead of Abel, whom Cain slew. And to Seth, to him also there was born a son; and he called his name Enos: then began men to call upon the name of the LORD** (Genesis 4:25,26). It seemed that for a while there was a change; people turned to God, but then they went back into sin. Again the devil took over in an awful way.

GOD REPENTED CREATING MAN

Some people wonder why God created man and woman if He knew they were going to sin. God told me personally one day that He didn't know they were going to sin or He never would have created them. He told me He wanted man and woman to trust Him one hundred percent, so He had to put one hundred percent trust in them. He sent them forth in His wisdom, in His knowledge, not in ignorance. He told them that if they sinned, they would die. They would no longer be His or belong to Him; they would be the property of the devil.

Eve saw that the forbidden fruit was pleasant to the

eyes, and she kept going to the tree. We don't know how long Eve went to that tree—a year, ten years, twenty years—we don't know how long it took the devil to deceive her. The devil does the same thing today. He makes things that are wrong, that are ugly in the eyes of God, seem pleasant and beautiful.

In the sixth chapter of Genesis we find that **GOD saw that the wickedness of man was great in the earth, and that every imagination of the thoughts of his heart was only evil continually. And it repented the LORD that he had made man on the earth, and it grieved him at his heart** (Genesis 6: 5,6).

Every thought of man's heart was evil continually. That's one reason we know we're almost to the end of our civilization today; the earth again is filled with evil thoughts and violence. We're almost to Rapture Day, and then the Tribulation Period will begin. Sin is everywhere throughout the world just as it was in Noah's day.

And the LORD said, I will destroy man whom I have created from the face of the earth; both man, and beast, and the creeping thing, and the fowls of the air; for it repenteth me that I have made them. But Noah found grace in the eyes of the LORD (Genesis 6:7,8). God had decided to destroy all civilization: That's how much He hated sin. But in His grace, He heard a voice crying out to Him. It was the voice of Noah.

NOAH FOUND GRACE

Noah found favor in the eyes of God. There was no sin in him; and, at that time, just eight souls had no sin; the rest died. Even children had to die because they were contaminated with the seed of sin; that's what one seed did, and you see the grave condition the world is in now. **And God said unto Noah, The end of all flesh is come before me; for the earth is filled with violence through them; and, behold, I will destroy them with the earth. Make thee an ark of gopher wood; rooms shalt thou make in the ark, and shalt pitch it within and without with pitch** (Genesis 6:13,14). Although God had had enough, He would preserve a root that was pure and holy—Noah.

The Noah family followed all directions in building the ark. God specified exactly how it was to be built: three stories high, representing the Father, Son, and Holy Ghost—the whole Godhead was in on it. **And this is the fashion which thou shalt make it of: The length of the ark shall be three hundred cubits** [450 feet], **the breadth of it fifty cubits** [75 feet], **and the height of it thirty cubits** [45 feet]. **A window shalt thou make to the ark,** and in a cubit shalt thou finish it above; and the door of the ark shalt thou set in the side thereof; with lower, second, and third stories shalt thou make it ... and thou shalt come into the ark, thou, and thy sons, and thy wife, and thy sons' wives with thee. And of every living thing of all flesh, two of every sort shalt thou bring into the ark, to keep them alive with thee; they shall be male and female. Of fowls after their kind, and of cattle after their kind, of every creeping thing of the earth after his kind, two of every sort shall come unto thee, to keep them alive. And take thou unto thee of all food that is eaten, and thou shalt gather it to thee; and it shall be for food for thee, and for them** (Genesis 6:15,16,18–21).

Every acquaintance of Noah, outside of his immediate family, was going to die, and be swept away. Homes, villages, towns would be destroyed—even livestock and the fowls of the air. What would his life be worth then? No doubt he thought it would be better for the Lord to take him and his family on to heaven, but he went ahead and did what the Lord asked. Noah was a humble man, obedient to the call of God; he built the ark for the glory of God, not himself.

People err when they build for themselves and not for God. Everything we do should be done for the glory of God. **Whether therefore ye eat, or drink, or whatsoever ye do, do all to the glory of God** (I Corinthians 10:31). **Thus did Noah; according to all that God commanded him, so did he** (Genesis 6:22).

And Noah went in, and his sons, and his wife, and his sons' wives with him, into the ark, because of the waters of the flood. And the waters prevailed, and were increased greatly upon the earth; and the ark went upon the face of the waters (Genesis 7:7,18).

After being in the ark over a year, the Noah family finally emerged, **and Noah builded an altar unto the LORD; and took of every clean beast, and of every clean fowl, and offered burnt offerings on the altar** (Genesis 8:20). You might think Noah would have built something for his family first, but no, he loved God more; Noah built an altar first. You do for God first when you love Him with all of your heart.

THE LAW HAS NO MERCY

When the Law was given, we saw the Lord separating sin on the left from righteousness on the right, unholiness on the left and holiness on the right. Everything was separated by God in the Law—left, right, left, right.

Achan was separated to the left. He confessed his sin: **Indeed I have sinned against the LORD God of Israel, and thus and thus have I done: When I saw among the spoils a goodly Bab-y-lo-nish garment, and two hundred shekels of silver, and a wedge of gold of fifty she-kels weight, then I coveted them, and took them; and, behold, they are hid in the earth in the midst of my tent, and the silver under it. And Joshua, and all Israel with him, took A-chan the son of Zerah, and the silver, and the garment, and the wedge of gold, and his sons, and his daughters, and his oxen, and his asses, and his sheep, and his tent, and all that he had: and they brought them unto the valley of A-chor. And Joshua said, Why hast thou troubled us? the LORD shall trouble thee this day. And all Israel stoned him with stones, and burned them with fire, after they had stoned them with stones** (Joshua 7:20,21,24,25).

Achan was a thief; and, to get that contamination out from among God's people, Achan, along with his wife, his children, his tent, his belongings, everything he had needed to be destroyed, wiped out completely. God brought judgment again and again in Old Testament days, although He loved the Israelite people as much as He has ever loved people in the New Testament dispensation.

Again and again the Law went into action and brought judgment immediately to the soul that sinned; sometimes people would die by the thousands. Seventy thousand died because David disobeyed God and numbered the army of the Lord. The Law was cruel. **And Satan stood up against Israel, and provoked David to number Israel. And God was displeased with this thing; therefore he smote Israel. So the LORD sent pestilence upon Israel: and there fell of Israel seventy thousand men** (I Chronicles 21:1,7,14).

Under the Law man didn't have the divine blood to use as we have it today, and God's judgment fell. The price had not yet been paid for man to stand as tall as the first Adam before the fall. Under the Law, God allowed some things, but not everything; some things He would not accept. In the New Testament we are reminded that **the times of this ignorance God winked at; but now commandeth all men every where to repent** (Acts 17:30). There's no longer any excuse for sin since Jesus came and paid the supreme price.

THE DEVIL WILL BE DESTROYED

The Lord is pouring out grace in abundance now because He's giving everything He has to save this human race on planet Earth. If all that heaven offers will not destroy sin, then the Lord knows He must get rid of sin's containers.

In the book of Revelation we find prophesied the destruction of Lucifer, the source of all evil. **And the devil that deceived them was cast into the lake of fire and brimstone, where the beast and the false prophet are, and shall be tormented day and night for ever and ever** (Revelation 20:10).

Until he fell from grace, the devil was beautiful and perfect in heaven. **Thou wast perfect in thy ways from the day that thou wast created, till iniquity was found in thee** (Ezekiel 28:15). Now Satan seeks to cause everyone to backslide. He lost his place in heaven, so he knows it can be done. In a perfect environment he beguiled the first Adam, enticed him to sin. When the second Adam came, the devil thought, *This will be easy. He's not in Eden; he's in my territory, on my ground. I'll deceive Him and make Him think I own all the kingdoms of the world.* But the devil couldn't deceive the second Adam any more than he can deceive you today who remain in God's light.

Although the devil has battled, fought, and warred against you—some battles going longer than others—you go deeper and deeper into the Spirit of God because you won't give in to the enemy. Never forget that you have the same divine blood that the second Adam had, the same divine blood that Adam and Eve had in the Garden. Born again, you have all power, all light: The Lord's giving it. As that light shineth you're receiving the knowledge of God for you in this final hour. **Arise, shine; for thy light is come, and the glory of the LORD is risen upon thee** (Isaiah 60:1).

RELATED TO HEAVEN

The Bride will not walk in the night in this last hour, saith the Lord. Knowing the ways of the Lord, she will walk in His love, His light, and His knowledge in perfection. She will know the Spirit of God, the spirit of man and the spirit of the devil, and she will be able to separate them as she goes forward in the same strength that Jesus used.

As a son or daughter of God, you're related to heaven just as much as the Only Begotten was related to heaven when He walked among men. He took on the fashion of man, lived with the same weaknesses, and fought the same devil, demons, and deceit. He faced it all and won. His faith is our faith when we are winners through Christ Jesus.

There is no need to look at those who are failing, those who are weak; look to Jesus. If you look at the weak, you'll begin to listen to what they have to say; but, if you look to Jesus, you will listen to Him.

When I was in the world I didn't look to Jesus much, but Jesus was kept before us children in the Angley family. Much praying went on in my home. I was made Jesus-conscious at home and in church. The Bible was the main book in our home, more important than newspapers, magazines, or schoolbooks. I was around people who believed, taught, and lived the Bible; and their example kept me from doing a lot of things I would have done otherwise.

GOD IS LONGSUFFERING

Just as the whole Godhead was involved in the creation of man and woman, so it is involved in the new civilization that Jesus brought. It was a long journey, thousands of years until Calvary, a plan of longsuffering and endurance for the Godhead that would cost heaven's heart.

We don't really understand the depths of the Lord's longsuffering. **But thou, O Lord, art a God full of compassion, and gracious, longsuffering, and plenteous in mercy and truth** (Psalm 86:15). We think one hundred and twenty years was a long time for Noah to be patient, but that's no time at all compared to these thousands of years God has waited for the redemption of all mankind and the end of sin.

God's Son bought the Church with His own blood, gave His life for it. At first, remember, the Early

Church was on fire to spread the Gospel; God saw the light of His Son in it and the power of the Holy Ghost directing it, leading it, teaching it the truths of God and giving it all power over any kind of devil. Then God had to watch as the Church fell into indifference and false doctrine. Oh, another blow to heaven!

Consider what God the Father, God the Son, and God the Holy Ghost have been through, what price they have paid because of sin! Imagine their grief when they hear people say that no one can live free from sin!

KING SAUL FAILED GOD

Saul was to be the first king of Israel; God gave him a new heart, a new spirit, and made his spirit like the spirit of the first Adam. The prophet Samuel told him about it: **And the spirit of the LORD will come upon thee** [Saul]**, and thou shalt prophesy with them, and shalt be turned into another man** (I Samuel 10:6). Yet Saul turned to the devil completely before he died, seeking knowledge from the devil. He knew better. **Then said Saul unto his servants, Seek me a woman that hath a familiar spirit, that I may go to her, and inquire of her. And his servants said to him, Behold, there is a woman that hath a familiar spirit at En-dor. And**

Saul disguised himself, and put on other raiment, and he went, and two men with him, and they came to the woman by night: and he said, I pray thee, divine unto me by the familiar spirit, and bring me him up, whom I shall name unto thee (I Samuel 28:7,8). But God had said: **And the soul that turneth after such as have familiar spirits, and after wizards, to go a-whoring after them, I will even set my face against that soul, and will cut him off from among his people** (Leviticus 20:6). In other words, God would destroy that soul in hell.

God is exacting in our lives. It's beyond my understanding why people let the devil deceive them into thinking they can commit willful sin and still go to God's heaven—or even walk with God here in this body!

CHAPTER 4

The Garments

The deceit garment is one of the awful garments that the devil and his people wear. It's like the devil himself; it looks like him and talks like him. You're either going to wear the garments of righteousness and holiness, or you're going to dress in the garments of the devil; and they are nothing but rags of unrighteousness, unholiness, filth, ungodliness, and contamination. What a stench they bring with them! God can't stand it; His nostrils can't bear it.

What garments are you wearing? Which wardrobe is yours? It's either Jesus' wardrobe or the devil's wardrobe. Make sure you're wearing the Jesus garments, or at times you may find yourself trying on something of the devil and then acting like the devil.

Remember, you must be able to separate the spirits. *The garments, saith the Lord, are one great way that you can separate the spirits.* The Lord carefully teaches us the garments of Jesus.

The Bible tells us to **Be ye angry, and sin not: let not the sun go down upon your wrath** (Ephesians 4:26). When you lose your temper, check to see if you are angry but without sin. Did you say anything harmful? You should have so much love in you that anger is destroyed before it can grow into hatred, envy, or strife; love destroys those things. Don't let anger linger; when it stays, you put on one of the garments of the devil—and sometimes more than one. The devil's garments are garments of hatred, injustice, dishonesty, impurity, uncleanness, and unholiness, to name a few.

The Lord has been dealing with me concerning the garments of the devil. If you commit sin, you reach for the garments of sin and make them a part of your spirit; you're wearing the garments of the devil. God's faith and love must be in your heart to keep sin out.

The Lord, in teaching about His Spirit, is also including the spiritual garments Jesus wore. His big wardrobe is filled with all the promises willed to you in the New Testament. The Lord has taught you much, and He's going to teach you much more about the devil because you must be able to recognize him in all his disguises—and he has plenty. If the devil can't deceive you with one garment, he'll try another. If he can't deceive you one way, he'll come from a different direction, and so it goes. The devil prides himself in being the arch deceiver. When he deceived the first man, he thought he had destroyed God's plan for the human race; but he didn't get it done.

GOD IS MORE THAN A MATCH FOR THE DEVIL

Evil thinks wrong; never depend on the devil's thinking. When the devil meets a true child of God, he meets more than his match because he is meeting God the Father, God the Son, and God the Holy Ghost. No contamination at all is in the family of God; the spirit of the born-new is just as pure as God's Spirit, the voice just as pure as His voice. That's the reason Jesus could say, **In my name shall they cast out devils . . . they shall lay hands on the sick, and they shall recover** (Mark 16:17,18).

The Bible tells us to lift up holy hands. **I will therefore that men pray every where, lifting up holy hands, without wrath and doubting** (I Timothy 2:8). I lift up a holy hand and the miracle takes place. God chose the laying on of hands for healing people, showing that God works through holiness—holy hands—and that man can and must be holy. One speck of willful sin in your heart means you're unholy. If the Holy Spirit lets you know you have sin, you must get it out of the way.

ABRAHAM HAD AMAZING FAITH

Abraham's faith went beyond Noah's faith. When the Lord told him to offer the son he had waited on for twenty-five years, he was willing to obey.

Isaac was about twelve years old when God told Abraham to take him to Mount Moriah and offer Isaac as a sacrifice unto Him. The Bible plainly tells us in the New Testament that Abraham knew if he killed Isaac that God would raise him up. **By faith Abraham, when he was tried, offered up Isaac; and he that had received the promises offered up his only begotten son, Of whom it was said, That in Isaac shall thy seed be called: Accounting that God was able to raise him up, even from the dead; from whence also he received him in a figure** (Hebrews 11:17–19). Abraham sacrificed Isaac in his own spirit and in the faithfulness of the Spirit of God that was in his heart.

God has branded my congregation at Grace Cathedral with faithfulness, saith the Lord. God is going on without the outer fringes, but the heart of my congregation is faithful. Without realizing it, many of them have come to the place that they would lay down their lives for the sake of Christ. Many today would walk out in front of a firing squad and be shot before they'd back down. Some of them may not think they have that much faith and courage, but they have more than they know. Faith can't be measured with feelings; faith is measured with the Word of the living God. The Word, the knowledge of God is your faith; accept it all.

[Abraham] **believed in the LORD; and he counted it to him for righteousness** (Genesis 15: 6). Only the Godhead is righteous within itself, and that righteousness has been expanded to us through the divine blood of Jesus. Abraham wore the garment of faith; he believed what the Lord had said. The divine blood went into his soul, and Abraham was indeed a son of God just like the first Adam once was. This reality of God is what people have overlooked; that's why we're to study the Word with the great teacher, the Holy Spirit Himself.

THEY STOOD TALL

Timothy received this letter from Paul: **I thank God, whom I serve from my forefathers with pure conscience, that without ceasing I have** remembrance of thee in my prayers night and day; Greatly desiring to see thee, being mindful of thy tears, that I may be filled with joy; When I call to remembrance the unfeigned faith that is in thee, which dwelt first in thy grandmother Lois, and thy mother Eunice; and I am persuaded that in thee also** (II Timothy 1:3–5). *That faith was in your grandmother, in your mother; and, Timothy, that faith is in you.* Wasn't that a beautiful statement? I'm sure Timothy pleased the Lord the rest of the journey.

Under the ordeal of knowing his dearest friend on earth was going to be beheaded, Timothy stood as tall as Jesus. When you stand as tall as Jesus you can take anything, suffer any persecutions. Jesus went into the deepest valleys of persecution and stood every test. He is our faith so we, too, can stand every test.

It doesn't matter what we must suffer to bring in the lost in this final hour, it doesn't matter the danger we're in; souls must be won and be made ready for the Rapture. Paul was forever in danger, even from his own countrymen, his own brethren in the flesh. People sought to kill him, but he stood as tall as Jesus and walked through the valleys just like Jesus did.

Paul wrote about some of his persecutions: **Of the Jews five times received I forty stripes save one.**

Thrice was I beaten with rods, once was I stoned, thrice I suffered shipwreck, a night and a day I have been in the deep; In journeyings often, in perils of waters, in perils of robbers, in perils by mine own countrymen, in perils by the heathen, in perils in the city, in perils in the wilderness, in perils in the sea, in perils among false brethren (II Corinthians 11:24–26).

Three times Paul cried for the Lord to take away the messenger of Satan that was following him everywhere he went. **And lest I should be exalted above measure through the abundance of the revelations, there was given to me a thorn in the flesh, the messenger of Satan to buffet me, lest I should be exalted above measure. For this thing I besought the Lord thrice, that it might depart from me** (II Corinthians 12:7,8).

Not until the third time Paul sought the Lord did he get his answer, and it wasn't what he expected. God's answer to Paul: **My grace is sufficient for thee: for my strength is made perfect in weakness** (II Corinthians 12:9). When God's grace is working in us, His strength is apparent to us and to all we come in contact with. God doesn't usually give the answers we expect to our questions. He is not a man, and He has definitely stated in His Word that He's not a man.

You must thoroughly know God and His ways. **For my thoughts are not your thoughts, neither are your ways my ways, saith the LORD. For as the heavens are higher than the earth, so are my ways higher than your ways, and my thoughts than your thoughts** (Isaiah 55:8,9). You can't out-think God; many have tried, but to no avail.

People you work with watch your life; they notice the inner strength you have that they don't have. They would like to have that strength; some seek the source and find that it's all God. That is the garment of strength, and it can bring them into the Kingdom as well.

Paul's life brought many people into the Kingdom. He was the greatest teacher of all the apostles in the New Testament, the greatest writer of all the writers. From the time the Lord knocked him down on the road to Damascus, Paul never turned and ran.

Peter in the Garden of Gethsemane wasn't where he ought to have been with the Lord, wasn't as close as he should have been in the love and faith of Jesus. He didn't have His overcoming power. His temper rose up, and he cut off a man's ear. **Then Simon Peter having a sword drew it, and smote the high priest's servant, and cut off his right ear. The servant's name was Malchus. Then said Jesus unto Peter, Put up thy sword into the sheath: the** cup which my Father hath given me, shall I not drink it** (John 18:10,11)? **And he** [Jesus] **touched his** [Malchus'] **ear, and healed him** (Luke 22:51).

When the Lord healed the servant's ear, it seems as if that would have caused Peter to be humble; but he went on to curse and deny the Lord.

OUR STRENGTH IS FROM THE LORD

I grow more and more humble before God as I see His miracles. When God is performing great miracles, again and again I would just like to fall on my face in holy sacredness. I'm in the cloud of His presence, surrounded by the glory of the Lord.

The Bible says the weak shall not say they are weak. **Let the weak say, I am strong** (Joel 3:10). Our testimony is that our strength comes through the Lord; and, in due season, the Lord will bring us out of the valley. **And let us not be weary in well-doing: for in due season we shall reap, if we faint not** (Galatians 6:9).

In prayer, the Psalmist let us know that **the eyes of the LORD are upon the righteous, and his ears are open unto their cry** (Psalm 34:15). But if you don't live free from sin, you are unholy and unrighteous. If you have any sin in you at all, your garments are contaminated; and you will never get through the gates of Glory that way.

Then said one unto him, Lord, are there few that be saved? And he said unto them, Strive to enter in at the strait gate: for many, I say unto you, will seek to enter in, and shall not be able. When once the master of the house is risen up, and hath shut to the door, and ye begin to stand without, and to knock at the door, saying, Lord, Lord, open unto us; and he shall answer and say unto you, I know you not whence ye are: Then shall ye begin to say, We have eaten and drunk in thy presence, and thou hast taught in our streets. But he shall say, I tell you, I know you not whence ye are; depart from me, all ye workers of iniquity. There shall be weeping and gnashing of teeth, when ye shall see Abraham, and Isaac, and Jacob, and all the prophets, in the kingdom of God, and you yourselves thrust out (Luke 13:23–28).

Jesus in no uncertain terms lets us know that anyone contaminated with sin cannot get through the gate of heaven. Even if you were to get to the gate, you couldn't pass through without being prepared. The garments of doubt, unbelief, and sin will shut the gates of Glory to you. Take the whole Word of God into your heart—the powerful, clean, holy Word—and keep any contamination and any unholy words out. Salvation is free; you paid absolutely nothing for it. Isaiah foretold the coming of it: **For** unto us a child is born, unto us a son is given: and the government shall be upon his shoulder: and his name shall be called Wonderful, Counsellor, The mighty God, The everlasting Father, The Prince of Peace** (Isaiah 9:6).

Isaiah prophesied the Virgin Birth. The greatness, the fullness of the Godhead would come to earth in a bodily form called Jesus: **Behold, a virgin shall conceive, and bear a son, and shall call his name Immanuel** (Isaiah 7:14).

THE BRIDE, A GOOD SOLDIER

This is the hour of the Bride, saith the Lord, the hour of her greatness, her crowning glory. She's going to march unafraid like a mighty army, showing no fear whatsoever; the Bride will overcome fear.

Fear comes momentarily to every good soldier, but that soldier takes strength from watching the bravery of his companions. It's amazing the strength soldiers get when they see someone facing death unafraid, and then they can go on. So will it be with us. *You will be an inspiration to other members of the bridal company, and you will go forth, saith the Lord, as a mighty army.*

The devil fears you and will try to make you fear him. Jesus didn't fear the devil, but the devil feared Him. That's the reason the devil left Jesus for a season. He wanted to get away from Jesus, to go off and think the matter over, to devise more tactics and then to return. However, nothing he tried on Jesus worked; and you don't have to fear what the devil might try on you, either.

Be a good soldier, the voice of the Lord through Paul was saying to Timothy: **Thou therefore, my son, be strong in the grace that is in Christ Jesus . . . endure hardness, as a good soldier of Jesus Christ** (II Timothy 2:1,3). Every member of the bridal company will be a good soldier.

INTO THE PIT GOES THE DEVIL

When this great power of the Holy Ghost takes over the whole earth for a thousand years, the devil will be helpless in the bottomless pit. **And I saw an angel come down from heaven, having the key of the bottomless pit and a great chain in his hand. And he laid hold on the dragon, that old serpent, which is the Devil, and Satan, and bound him a thousand years, And cast him into the bottomless pit, and shut him up, and set a seal upon him, that he should deceive the nations no more, till the thousand years should be fulfilled: and after that he must be loosed a little season** (Revelation 20:1–3).

Realize what a bluffer the devil is! God's grace

is definitely sufficient for you. He has more than enough strength and power for all the battles you will fight between here and Rapture Day. He has more than enough health and healing and more than enough power to guide every step you will have time to make.

REASON WITH GOD

Paul told one church to take on the mind of Jesus. **Let this mind be in you, which was also in Christ Jesus** (Philippians 2:5). Your mind is to be like the mind of Christ.

Come now, and let us reason together (Isaiah 1:18). Spend time reasoning with God; let Him do the talking. Don't beg Him for answers. Just listen and He will reason with you. Through the spiritual senses you can hear the rustle of His garments and know His moving, His working. The Bride will respond to the Lord's moves, His walk, His talk; and she'll choose His thoughts, His ways.

As you choose God's thoughts, you are refusing to allow the spirits of depression to linger in your mind. Winning more and more of the battles of the mind, you recognize and reject the spirit that brings the thoughts that cause those battles.

Anyone can be depressed for a short time; however, to stay depressed, to put it on as a garment and wear it means you're not wearing one of Jesus' garments. Depression or oppression may come momentarily; but because you recognize those garments, you refuse them, and they won't linger. Jesus always recognized through the Holy Spirit whether a spirit came from heaven, from the devil, or from people. Jesus knew the spirits; **he knew all men** (John 2: 24).

When every step is a truth step, we don't have to move as though we're walking on eggs on our way to heaven. We let the devil know we mean business. Because our garments are covered with the blood, we're not afraid of him. The devil can't stand the blood and is not about to touch it; he knows it means his destruction. All you have to do is stay under the blood. The devil is forever trying to get your attention, to get you to come out from under the blood. Take a lesson from Adam and Eve. The devil tantalized them until he got them to come out from the divine blood and step into his territory of disobedience. There he snared them.

BE MINDFUL OF YOUR GARMENTS

If you'll follow and believe what the Lord is giving you, you will have the knowledge of sin and righteousness in a way you've never had it before. Be mindful of the garments you're wearing; be alert

Chapter 4: The Garments

and watching for Jesus to come in your day. He's coming for a people who are watching for Him, who are not going to be reaching over for one of the devil's garments; they know if they do, they'll miss the Rapture.

The devil makes his garments look beautiful. In Eden the fruit was pleasant to the eyes—that's how the devil attracted Eve. But the devil is all false, and his lights are false.

Consider the beautiful Hollywood lights. As kids growing up, we thought that was one of the greatest heights to climb to—the lights of Hollywood, the lights of the stage, the lights of this world, the dancing, the swing bands. We didn't think about the drinking and the drugs. Once in a while we would hear of someone being a drug addict in New York City, but we didn't dream of ever meeting one. Now they may live next door.

Today, we see people climbing what the world calls the ladder of success, but many of them are in hell today. Some commit suicide, and others die horrible deaths. Not using their talents for God, they sell their souls to the devil for the lust of the flesh. Theirs isn't a ladder to success after all; it's a ladder to destruction. They climb it only to find ashes and dust. Realizing they have thrown their lives away, they feel there is nothing to live for—how pathetic!

If someone can get to them with the truth, they can find the Lord; but the Christian world has failed the human race.

The Gospel of Jesus Christ has always been strong enough to defeat Lucifer and all his devils. The lack of strength comes when people won't live according to the Gospel but rather live according to their own opinions with the devil's opinions mixed in.

When you function through opinions, you may not realize that the devil's influence is behind those opinions. In living for God, take your opinions to Him before you dare use them on anyone else. You're responsible for your opinions, responsible for the garments you choose to wear.

CHAPTER 5

Ten Commandments

Study and carefully weigh everything the Lord tells you; weigh the scriptures again and again, for you learn much that way. When you run across something in the Bible you want more light on, study the first time it's mentioned. Notice, I go back to Eden again and again. When you go back to the first time any subject is mentioned, it sheds more light on other scriptures. It's a beautiful way to learn.

THE JUDGMENTS OF GOD

An angel told Lot the city he lived in was about to be destroyed. **For we will destroy this place, because the cry of them is waxen great before the face of the LORD; and the LORD hath sent us**

to destroy it (Genesis 19:13).

Be mindful of God's wrath, God's judgments that He has poured out since the time man was driven from Eden. There's much to study and to think about: the sorrow, the heartache that people endured. God found few He could really trust. He found Noah, his family, and Abraham to be trustworthy; and He was able to trust Lot part of the time, although later more than in the beginning.

We don't know how close to God Lot was, but we know he got into deep trouble when he separated from Abraham and took his family into Sodom. Lot, the Bible tells us in the New Testament, was vexed. **Just Lot,** [was] **vexed with the filthy conversation of the wicked: (For that righteous man dwelling among them, in seeing and hearing, vexed his righteous soul from day to day with their unlawful deeds;)** (II Peter 2:7,8).

Two angels came to warn Lot that Sodom and Gomorrah would be destroyed. They told Lot and his family: **Arise, take thy wife, and thy two daughters, which are here; lest thou be consumed in the iniquity of the city. And while he lingered, the men laid hold upon his hand, and upon the hand of his wife, and upon the hand of his two daughters; the LORD being merciful unto him: and they brought him forth, and set him with-**

out the city. And it came to pass, when they had brought them forth abroad, that he said, Escape for thy life; look not behind thee, neither stay thou in all the plain; escape to the mountain, lest thou be consumed** (Genesis 19:15–17).

Lot had a righteous soul; the two daughters must have also had righteous souls. **Then the LORD rained upon Sodom and upon Go-mor-rah brimstone and fire from the LORD out of heaven; And he overthrew those cities, and all the plain, and all the inhabitants of the cities, and that which grew upon the ground. But his** [Lot's] **wife looked back from behind him, and she became a pillar of salt** (Genesis 19:24–26).

God doesn't tell us why Lot's wife was so drawn to the world. God just wants us to know that judgment fell on her, and He had a right to do it. God was strict even before the Law was given. Lot's wife wasn't in a good spiritual condition; in fact, the angel holding on to her had to drag her out of the city. Only one look back and Lot's wife was killed.

This is a true story of God's judgment. There was no mercy left, no Jesus to keep her holding onto the Father to give her another chance; so judgment fell upon her. Lot's wife blasphemed against the Spirit of God. When you blaspheme against the Spirit of God, there's no more mercy for you.

Some people are going to look back no matter what, backsliding right up to the moment the Rapture takes place. How sad it will be for those who take that one last look back and suddenly find themselves left in the Tribulation Period!

Haste thee, escape thither; for I cannot do any thing till thou be come thither (Genesis 19:22). The Lord cannot bring all-out judgment until the Bride is out of here; remember this. But when the Bride is raptured, all hell will turn loose on earth. People left behind will experience the drastic and terrible difference between the mercy of the Church Dispensation and the dispensation without mercy.

This dispensation of God's mercy is about to end after two thousand years. How much gratitude for His mercy has been shown? How many souls has the Lord reaped? The majority of people who have lived these past two thousand years are in hell today.

People are careless, doing things they know are wrong and thinking that, since judgment doesn't immediately fall, they'll get by. However, when judgment does come, it will bring eternal death; God will have nothing more to do with them, for they will have sealed their doom.

Why does God put up with what He does today? It's because mercy is standing between Him and the pouring-out of judgment, and that mercy is Jesus.

God didn't give this mercy under the Law.

For over four hundred years in Old Testament days, God saw His people worshiping idol gods in Egypt. Few had really served God, and even fewer had taught their children about God; so generation after generation in Egypt had no real teaching of Jehovah God and Creation. In the wilderness the Israelites made a golden calf and judgment fell. Moses rebuked Israel for their sin: **Ye have sinned a great sin: and now I will go up unto the LORD; peradventure I shall make an atonement for your sin** (Exodus 32:30). Because of Israel's disobedience, God killed thousands and thousands; we have no way to number them all. God has let people get by with so much in this Grace Dispensation that many are deceived. But the cry is still going forth: The soul that sinneth shall die. God is just as serious as ever.

And the LORD said unto Moses, Whosoever hath sinned against me, him will I blot out of my book. And the LORD plagued the people, because they made the calf, which Aaron made (Exodus 32:33,35).

BE YE HOLY

Surely you've read the story again and again of God coming down on Mount Sinai to give Moses the Ten Commandments. God wrote them with His finger; that's how much He loved man and woman and wanted to draw them to Him. It was a letter of *thou shalt nots*. Some think of that as judgment; no, the Ten Commandments are a great love letter letting the people know what was unacceptable to God.

Sanctify yourselves therefore, and be ye holy: for I am the LORD your God (Leviticus 20:7). The Lord gave the Ten Commandments so that people would have a standard of holiness to live by.

Think about sin, righteousness, and the Law. Study the Ten Commandments; let them shed plenty of light on what God wants you to understand concerning the Spirit of God, the spirit of the devil and the spirit of man.

The Ten Commandments begin with: **Thou shalt have no other gods before me** (Exodus 20:3). Don't make this world your god, don't bow down to this world. God's demand for holiness is the same today as it was then: *Thou shalt not sin, thou shalt not.* The Lord saw that offering the blood of animals wouldn't keep man out of sin, and He was displeased. **For it is not possible that the blood of bulls and of goats should take away sins. Wherefore when he cometh into the world, he saith, Sacrifice and offering thou wouldest not, but a body hast thou prepared me: In burnt offerings and sacrifices**

for sin thou hast had no pleasure (Hebrews 10: 4–6). On the Day of Atonement, people did well to stay out of sin just that one day; then, it was back into sin, and judgments would fall.

God can hate as much as He can love. He works with man as long as He can, and that's it; He reaches His limit. God went a limited distance with man in giving the Law; but, when He gave Jesus, He went all the way. There's no place to go beyond Calvary. God gave everything, gave us the heart of heaven—His heart—the heart of all His love, grace, peace, direction, strength. He supplied all His divine blood and nothing was left; that's the reason God turned His back when Christ was crying on the cross: **My God, my God, why hast thou forsaken me** (Mark 15:34)? Having no more to give, God had to black out the scene and turn His back on His Only Begotten so He wouldn't come down in judgment and destroy the plan of salvation. Oh, how much He loved us!

Thou shalt not make unto thee any graven image, or any likeness of any thing that is in heaven above, or that is in the earth beneath, or that is in the water under the earth (Exodus 20:4). People have all kinds of gods today; having love for so many things, they are without love for God.

If you love anyone or anything better than you love

God, Jesus tells you that you're not fit to be His disciple: **He that loveth father or mother more than me is not worthy of me: and he that loveth son or daughter more than me is not worthy of me. And he that taketh not his cross, and followeth after me is not worthy of me** (Matthew 10:37–38).

Thou shalt not take the name of the LORD thy God in vain; for the LORD will not hold him guiltless that taketh his name in vain (Exodus 20:7). People curse, swear, and think they're all right. They're not all right; Jesus is holding back the wrath of the Father, holding back destruction. When He steps aside, it will be over and done; God's judgment will fall. God is very close to the end of His longsuffering.

We've never seen so much destruction on earth—through people, the elements, and other ways—as is taking place today. The devil is in people, making them want to destroy others. It's a perilous hour if you don't have God; it's dangerous to live one moment without Him. God is our only hope, but the devil makes people think they'll be all right without Him. They take God's name in vain, and He hates it, despises it; there's eternal death for it and for all sin.

KEEP EVERY DAY HOLY

God doesn't want us to forsake the assembling of ourselves together. **Not forsaking the assembling of ourselves together, as the manner of some is; but exhorting one another: and so much the more, as ye see the day approaching** (Hebrews 10:25).

In Old Testament days, the Sabbath was to be holy. **Ye shall keep the sabbath therefore; for it is holy unto you: every one that defileth it shall surely be put to death: for whosoever doeth any work therein, that soul shall be cut off from among his people** (Exodus 31:14). Old Testament Israelites were put to death for defiling the Sabbath, not keeping it holy. Although the Lord told people under the Law to live holy, there were some things God overlooked in the Old Testament, but no longer. Now we're called to repentance for anything sinful. It's a must that we keep every day holy and consecrate ourselves to the Lord. That Sabbath day represents all our days.

Some people try to drag us back under the Law, but I don't want to be under the Law. I didn't get delivered from my sins and born new under the Law; I was born a new creature under grace. When I found the second Adam, Jesus, He made me over, re-created me in the image of God like He made the first Adam, like He made you new who have been born again. That's the reason the message to Nicodemus was so important, **Ye must be born again** (John 3:7).

There are those who claim that the Sabbath is the mark of the beast. They claim to know much about prophecy, but who would want to hear their prophecies?—Only the deceived. The Sabbath is not the mark of the beast; that's not what the Bible says. The Sabbath has nothing to do with the book of Revelation, but living unholy on any day does. Do you see how lopsided the devil makes people? Man was created to stay on course, on track; and he was meant to live in holiness and righteousness all the days of his life. It's taken all that heaven can afford to make it possible for people to be in the image of God, to be born again.

HONOR GODLY PARENTS

Honour thy father and thy mother: that thy days may be long upon the land which the LORD thy God giveth thee (Exodus 20:12). There's little honor for Christian mothers and fathers today. The courts can take away children at the drop of a hat; it's the spirit of the Antichrist robbing people of their children. A child can pick up a telephone, dial a number and have the police come into the house and arrest the parents. The children then go to foster homes. This is just another sign that we're coming to the end.

The Bible says to **train up a child in the way he should go: and when he is old, he will not depart from it** (Proverbs 22:6). It also says, **He that spareth his rod hateth his son: but he that loveth him chasteneth him betimes** (Proverbs 13:24). Many people hate their children today and can't stand to be around them. They can't even correct them the Bible way with any liberty. At one time mothers and fathers gave authority to the schools to discipline their children however they saw fit. Teachers were held in high esteem in the home. The values that some of us grew up with and loved have almost completely disappeared, even before we get out of here.

We're losing freedom fast in America. It's a disgrace how the name of Jesus Christ is misused. The Bible has been taken out of our schools, paving the way for the devil to be in them. Witchcraft can be taught in school but not the Bible. We're in a bigger mess than many realize. When you see how people live today in comparison to the teachings of the Gospel of Jesus Christ, you can understand the trouble we're in.

LIKE THE DAYS OF NOAH

The Lord said the day of His coming would be like the days of Noah and the days of Sodom and Gomorrah. **And as it was in the days of Noe, so shall it be also in the days of the Son of man. They did eat, they drank, they married wives, they were given in marriage, until the day that Noe entered into the ark, and the flood came, and destroyed them all. Likewise also as it was in the days of Lot; they did eat, they drank, they bought, they sold, they planted, they builded; But the same day that Lot went out of Sodom it rained fire and brimstone from heaven, and destroyed them all** (Luke 17:26–29). Hideous sins are everywhere today. The devil has even been able to spew them into our schoolrooms and onto our children.

Open your eyes to God the Father, God the Son, and God the Holy Ghost. Open your eyes to all truth today; get rid of your opinions and take the opinions and thoughts of God. I desire to think like God thinks; I want Him to take over my mind and give me the very thoughts of His heart. The Bride is to live in such a way that she can have the thoughts of God.

In this hour of darkness, fear is settling down all over the earth. Why?—Because the Ten Commandments and the Jesus-love commandments are all being broken. There are people who don't want any representation of the birth of Christ on government property or in the schools, and they don't want God mentioned on our money. They're trying to do away with everything concerning God, and God is about ready to send them to hell to get rid of them, to close them off and throw away the key, so to speak. When they're cast into the lake of fire, God will wipe them out of His memory forever. God has the power to forget people He doesn't want to remember; to Him it will be as though they had never existed. **And whosoever was not found written in the book of life was cast into the lake of fire** (Revelation 20:15).

And I saw a new heaven and a new earth: for the first heaven and the first earth were passed away; and there was no more sea. And I John saw the holy city, new Jerusalem, coming down from God out of heaven, prepared as a bride adorned for her husband (Revelation 21:1,2). The Lord is going to have His Eden right here on planet Earth the way He planned it. He had planned for this entire planet to be an Eden, not just one Garden. Had sin not entered, the sons and daughters of Adam and Eve would have had a paradise to live in. After Adam and Eve had proven themselves by staying in the image of God, the Lord would have destroyed the devil, cast him into destruction, and that would have been the end of him. But it didn't work that way. Throughout the ages the Lord has given man and woman every chance to turn to Him, but soon that free choice will be gone completely.

MORE COMMANDMENTS FROM GOD

Thou shalt not kill (Exodus 20:13). It's hard to tell how many people have been or will be murdered on planet Earth today. People are so devil-possessed that they will kill anyone: mother, daddy, entire families, and even people they don't know. Not too long ago, a man and a boy randomly shot thirteen people. Under the Law they would have been put to death for their crimes, but now many don't believe in capital punishment. God believed in it and still does.

Do you believe like God? From cover to cover find out what God's Bible teaches so you will know whether or not you believe the way God believes.

Preacher, I don't think anyone should be put to death.

God disagrees; remember, He has killed people by the thousands. Learn what God is like; He's the God who will either destroy you or take you to live with Him in love as the eternal ages roll. God has a mighty hand of mercy and a mighty hand of judgment.

Most people on earth today stand for nothing pure or holy. The world church has taken over to a great extent, and only the Holy Ghost through the Bride of Christ is holding back the judgments of the Tribulation Period.

You and others like you throughout the earth who are living holy are the reason that God's wrath is being held back. But when the Bride is taken out in the Rapture, it will be like a great dam has burst; the waters of tribulation will fill the earth in moments of time. My Lord and my God! We have no idea what's ahead when it comes to killings or parents being dishonored. We're just getting samples of these things now.

Thou shalt not commit adultery (Exodus 20: 14). Adultery is becoming accepted in our society, so much so that even some Christians are influenced by it.

When I was growing up, divorce was an ugly thing I seldom heard about, but times have changed. Today divorce and remarriage are common. Couples don't bother to go to the Bible to see if they're free to remarry. This disregard for God's Word started in Hollywood years ago; television has picked it up and it's gone like the wind all over the world. Young people, keep yourselves pure, clean, and holy. That's what God wants and expects of you.

Some parents can't talk to their children about sex. In a holy, godly way parents should be able to answer any question their children ask about sex. If they don't, the children are going to learn about it in a dirty way. When children don't get information about sex in the home, they get it in school or somewhere else. And when they get that information in other places, it doesn't come holy the way it should be presented in the home. The Bible explains it God's way, a holy way. **Marriage is honourable in all, and the bed undefiled: but whoremongers and adulterers God will judge** (Hebrews 13:4). It's sinful to have sex outside of marriage. Always remember: *The soul that sinneth shall die.*

In the New Testament we read that people were going to stone a woman who was caught in the act of adultery. But mercy had come to planet Earth in a man called Jesus, and He stopped them. **And the scribes and Pharisees brought unto him a woman taken in adultery; and when they had set her in the midst, They say unto him, Master, this woman was taken in adultery, in the very act. Now Moses in the law commanded us, that such should be stoned: but what sayest thou? This they said, tempting him, that they might have to accuse him. But Jesus stooped down, and with his finger wrote on the ground, as though he heard**

them not. So when they continued asking him, he lifted up himself, and said unto them, He that is without sin among you, let him first cast a stone at her. And again he stooped down, and wrote on the ground. And they which heard it, being convicted by their own conscience, went out one by one, beginning at the eldest, even unto the last: and Jesus was left alone, and the woman standing in the midst (John 8:3–9).

This is the only time we have record that Christ wrote, and I guarantee you that He wrote the names of the women these men had been with. He didn't have to preach to them; He just kept writing, and it got rid of the accusers. They recognized the fact that Jesus knew they were guilty. They were afraid He'd turn on them and cry, *There's a guilty one; let's get him, too!* Jesus could have said, *Why not kill them all today? I'll cast the first stone because I'm pure and clean!*

Under the Ten Commandments this woman caught in the act of adultery was due to die—and her accusers were, too. None of them were innocent, so they dropped their stones quietly, hoping Christ wouldn't notice; and they backed away a few yards before they turned and ran for cover.

When Jesus had lifted up himself, and saw none but the woman, he said unto her, Woman, where

are those thine accusers** (John 8:10)? Under the Law, accusers had to witness against a person before he or she could be put to death. **Hath no man condemned thee? She said, No man, Lord. And Jesus said unto her, Neither do I condemn thee: go, and sin no more** (John 8:10,11). This was not the voice of the Ten Commandments, this was the voice of the Gospel of Jesus Christ. He was saying, *My blood washes away this sin of yours. I now make you new, give you a new life; but sin no more.* If it had been impossible for her to go forth and never sin again, Christ would have preached false doctrine when He was here.

ADULTERY OF THE HEART

People close their eyes to the judgments of God and then claim they can sin and still go to heaven. That isn't what Jesus said in the Sermon on the Mount: **Ye have heard that it was said by them of old time, Thou shalt not commit adultery: But I say unto you, That whosoever looketh on a woman to lust after her hath committed adultery with her already in his heart** (Matthew 5:27,28). Jesus is saying that if a married man looks upon a woman with the intent of having intercourse with her if he has the opportunity, that spirit of adultery is in him—that spirit of the devil—and he has really committed adultery in his heart.

Death is pronounced upon adulterers. Do people pay attention to what God is saying? Do they care? Couples separate over nothing and then marry someone else. Jesus said, **Whosoever shall put away his wife, except it be for fornication, and shall marry another, committeth adultery: and whoso marrieth her which is put away doth commit adultery** (Matthew 19:9). This is truth, the Gospel truth that Jesus brought. Many today commit adultery and have no conscience about it.

PEOPLE WERE PUT TO DEATH FOR STEALING

Thou shalt not steal (Exodus 20:15). Don't you know you'll go to hell for stealing? I've wondered whether some people think they will get through the gate of Glory with what they've stolen.

We might as well face facts. Stealing a penny is the same as stealing a thousand dollars in the eyes of God. If you rob one person, it's the same as robbing a bank in the eyes of God; and you'll go to hell for it. If you steal from your mother or dad in your home, it's no different than your going down the street and robbing a neighbor. You don't have to steal a mule to go to hell; stealing is stealing, and the Lord said *thou shalt not steal.*

The Law, I say again, was cruel; people were put

to death for stealing. Trials weren't included in the Law, nor will there be any trials at the White Throne Judgment, no lawyers to plead your case. God goes by true facts, and God gave His holy prophets in the Old Testament the truth about people.

LIARS GO TO HELL

Some so-called Christians will lie if they are cornered. People have lied to me, and I knew they were lying. My mother taught me that a liar can't tell a story exactly the same every time. Have you ever noticed that? I remember a man I was doing business with who would lie. All I had to do was backtrack on his story, let him tell that story again, and guess what? It wasn't the same.

People telling little white lies are not exempt; all lies are damnable. The Bible says all liars will be cast into the lake of fire. **But the fearful, and unbelieving, and the abominable, and murderers, and whoremongers, and sorcerers, and idolaters, and all liars, shall have their part in the lake which burneth with fire and brimstone: which is the second death** (Revelation 21:8).

How can you be baptized in the Spirit of truth and have the Spirit of truth dwelling in you, if you don't always tell the truth? Willfully lying is deceit, willful sin. Never forget: *The soul that sinneth shall die*. First you die spiritually, and then you die in that eternal living death called hell as the endless ages roll.

Deceit is ugly, nasty, hellish; there won't be any of it in heaven. The Lord cast out the devil and all his angels because He found one little seed of deceit. **And there was war in heaven: Michael and his angels fought against the dragon; and the dragon fought and his angels, And prevailed not; neither was their place found any more in heaven. And the great dragon was cast out, that old serpent, called the Devil, and Satan, which deceiveth the whole world: he was cast out into the earth, and his angels were cast out with him** (Revelation 12: 7–9). God cast them out of heaven.

God is serious about holy living, but whether or not you live holy is up to you. You can choose to be careless with your tongue or you can use the love bridle.

FALSE WITNESSES

Thou shalt not bear false witness against thy neighbour (Exodus 20:16). Think how many lives have been destroyed by false witnesses, how many homes have been wrecked and ruined, how many godly people have had their character tarnished by lies. Jesus spoke the truth and yet He was accused of all kinds of offenses, even of being devil-possessed. But Jesus didn't run after the liars; He was busy serving truth. You can't run after liars either.

But, Preacher, someone lied about me.

Well, they'll go to hell if they don't get forgiveness for it.

DON'T COVET

Thou shalt not covet thy neighbour's house, thou shalt not covet thy neighbour's wife, nor his manservant, nor his maidservant, nor his ox, nor his ass, nor any thing that is thy neighbour's (Exodus 20:17). Many people want what others have rather than saying, *Lord, I'm glad you're blessing them.* They're jealous; they covet. I've seen people in the congregation become hurt because they felt God loved someone else better than He loved them. *Look how the Lord blesses them, and look what I'm going through,* they complain.

They need to look at what Jesus endured; He's the example of sufferings and paying the price. Look at Him instead of what others have.

Some people are always looking for a tidbit—or more—of gossip about another, even about their brothers and sisters in Christ. Always ready to criticize, they think anything that puts another person in a bad light is something they just must tell; they feel important telling it.

That's not godly; in fact, there's no love of God in it at all. People will go—and have gone—to hell for talebearing. **A talebearer revealeth secrets: but he that is of a faithful spirit concealeth the matter** (Proverbs 11:13). **The words of a talebearer are as wounds, and they go down into the innermost parts of the belly** (Proverbs 18:8). In the New Testament, the Bible also lets you know that hell awaits talebearers and gossipers. **And the tongue is a fire, a world of iniquity: so is the tongue among our members, that it defileth the whole body, and setteth on fire the course of nature; and it is set on fire of hell** (James 3:6).

Hell waits for everyone and everything unholy. Nothing but holiness is in heaven, and never will anything be there but holiness.

We can't listen to the world, to those who have twisted the truths of God and tried their best to destroy Him and all He stands for. These efforts come from the spirit of the devil who claimed he would ascend above the Most High, that he would be like Him and have power like Him. But the Lord said: **How art thou fallen from heaven, O Lucifer, son of the morning! how art thou cut down to the ground, which didst weaken the nations! For thou hast said in thine heart, I will ascend into heaven,**

I will exalt my throne above the stars of God: I will sit also upon the mount of the congregation, in the sides of the north: I will ascend above the heights of the clouds; I will be like the most High. Yet thou shalt be brought down to hell, to the sides of the pit. They that see thee shall narrowly look upon thee, and consider thee, saying, Is this the man that made the earth to tremble, that did shake kingdoms (Isaiah 14:12–16)?

TAKE YOUR STAND

Let God be your influence, not family or friends. Take your stand and be counted in the family of God. Some of you will have to grow a mighty strong backbone to be able to stand so that your family won't weaken you. Even loved ones can be like fiery darts of the enemy coming after you, pouring their condemnation on your head to hinder you. Stand tall against everything and everyone unlike God. The Bible tells us to **mark the perfect man, and behold the upright: for the end of that man is peace** (Psalm 37:37).

Why give over to critics? Why let them belittle your experience with God or your salvation? You don't have to put up with that. You're in the arena, and many times the devouring lions are right in your own home. Jesus lets you know in the Bible that He didn't come to bring families together; He came to separate good and evil, truth and false. **Think not that I am come to send peace on earth: I came not to send peace, but a sword. For I am come to set a man at variance against his father, and the daughter against her mother, and the daughter in law against her mother in law. And a man's foes shall be they of his own household** (Matthew 10:34–36).

Either you're in the truth or you're in deceit, serving God or not serving God, living holy or not living holy. Either you're in God's image or you're not; God is your Father or else the devil is your father. There are just two choices—one good, one bad. If you're not on your way to heaven, you're on your way to hell.

The deceiving spirit of man is so easily believed that, if you're not careful, you'll have a tendency to believe people before you believe the Lord, taking people's thoughts for this hour rather than taking the thoughts of the Lord. Do you let people cause you to doubt that we live in the sunset of the Church Dispensation? The endtime signs are screaming loudly enough for you to hear clearly even if you only casually listen.

You can't yield to the opinions of people when you yield to the truth of God through the Holy Spirit, because the Holy Spirit is truth. The Spirit of truth is the only one who can prepare you to be changed in a moment, in the twinkling of an eye, the only one who can enable you to escape in the Rapture just before all hell turns loose in the great Tribulation Period. But before the Lord gives the earth into the hands of the devil, He's going to take the Bride out of here; nothing will destroy that plan. Be warned that the devil will try to plant unbelief in you in every way he can. What can you do?—Decide that there's no room in your spirit for one tiny seed of doubt, not one. Believe the truth, accept the truth and don't waver.

MEET THE QUALIFICATIONS

Let nothing take your eyes off God. Claim God's promise of supply: **My God shall supply all your need according to his riches in glory by Christ Jesus** (Philippians 4:19). God is saying, *I will supply; I will give to you.* Your part is to meet the qualification of each promise, and then you can claim any and all the promises, even this big promise: **They that wait upon the LORD shall renew their strength; they shall mount up with wings as eagles; they shall run, and not be weary; and they shall walk, and not faint** (Isaiah 40:31).

Patiently wait for the fulfillment of the promise

after you've met the qualification. **For ye have need of patience, that, after ye have done the will of God, ye might receive the promise** (Hebrews 10: 36).

How do you qualify for a promise? You had to meet certain qualifications in order to graduate from high school or college, whether you wanted to or not. You were told what was required, and you had to pass those subjects to qualify for your diploma. God's promises are yours, but to qualify you have to live holy, trust God, and claim them!

GOD HAD A PLAN

The Ten Commandments were hard; they stung. What would you have done under the Law? How would you have handled those commandments? Would you have been one killed for your disobedience? The judgments of God should warn you that even under grace you must be very careful to stay in the newness of life, the new and living way that Jesus brought.

After all that the Lord had done in giving the Ten Commandments, how disappointed He was! But He didn't let that disappointment rob Him. No, He never gave up even when He cursed the ground, drove Adam and Eve from His presence and had no more fellowship with them. How pathetic! God cried; He hadn't thought that man would fall, but in His disappointment He worked out a great plan to get man back to Eden. Since all born outside of Eden would no longer be born in the image of God, what plan would God have to come up with? It was a plan in which people could become exactly like the man and woman God had created in His image in the first place. I'm sure the Godhead talked about it, and the Son of God volunteered to be our holy sacrifice. It's the blood of Jesus that wipes out all sin, makes you a new person on the inside with the same heart you would have had if you had been born in Eden—a heart pure, clean, holy and obedient to God.

A HOLY SACRIFICE

What kind of sacrifice will the Lord accept in grace?—Only a holy sacrifice. **I Beseech you therefore, brethren, by the mercies of God, that ye present your bodies a living sacrifice, holy, acceptable unto God, which is your reasonable service** (Romans 12:1).

Outside of Eden you have to overcome all the spirits of the demons that surround you all your life. If those demons get inside, you need to be delivered from demon possession.

No longer do people have to wait outside a little tabernacle to be made free of sin as was required under the Law, they can come to Calvary and be set free. The veil in the temple was rent from top to bottom, signifying that the Law was no longer in effect. The price had been paid and now it was grace. **And Jesus cried with a loud voice, and gave up the ghost. And the veil of the temple was rent in twain from the top to the bottom. And when the centurion, which stood over against him, saw that he so cried out, and gave up the ghost, he said, Truly this man was the Son of God** (Mark 15:37–39).

Under grace, man and woman can **come boldly unto the throne of grace, that we may obtain mercy, and find grace to help in time of need** (Hebrews 4:16). The blood of Jesus brought the throne of God within our faith-blood reach right here on planet Earth. Born again, we are the new creation, not the old. We were not born in the image of God in the physical birth; in that wretched, wrecked condition, we needed a Savior. We had to be born new, had to have the second birth.

Aren't you glad that the second Adam came to earth and won for us? Aren't you glad that you have come into deliverance?—into peace, joy, and freedom from sin? There is no Day of Atonement each year for us; the atonement that Jesus made is ours all the time.

Because of the nail-riven hands, you'll find answers for your children and strength for the journey daily. Through the nail-riven hands you can have the physical health needed. It's still the will of God, just like it was in Eden, that you be in good health. **Beloved, I wish above all things that thou mayest prosper and be in health, even as thy soul prospereth** (III John 1:2).

GOD'S LONGSUFFERING IS ALMOST OVER

In the beginning in Eden, the thoughts of Adam and Eve were the same as God's thoughts. But when they fell, they went as low as the devil himself, becoming contaminated and repulsive to God.

God can't look upon sin. In His longsuffering, He has waited for sin's destruction. Now His longsuffering is about over, and *God is counting on His people, saith the Lord.* He's brought people from the East, the West, the North, and the South, just as He told this servant years ago that He would. He showed me the great rockets of miracle power going forth from Grace Cathedral to the ends of the earth, striking the sky and sending stars tumbling. The Lord let me know that the stars represented souls, souls that I would win for Him.

There's no need to be afraid of this hour; the things I'm telling you are not to put the devil's fear in you but to put God's fear in all of us. Godly fear is respect for God. Respect His Book above all other books; respect His thoughts, His plans and His promises to us. That's the godly fear the Lord wants you to have.

People may criticize you; but, remember, that although they criticized Jesus, He gave them the truth. They criticized Paul, but he still gave them the truth. When you give people the truth of God, you're not responsible if they go to hell; but, if you compromise, you're responsible. Didn't the Lord tell Ezekiel to warn the wicked? Yes, He did. **Son of man, I have made thee a watchman unto the house of Israel: therefore hear the word at my mouth, and give them warning from me. When I say unto the wicked, Thou shalt surely die; and thou givest him not warning, nor speakest to warn the wicked from his wicked way, to save his life; the same wicked man shall die in his iniquity; but his blood will I require at thine hand. Yet if thou warn the wicked, and he turn not from his wickedness, nor from his wicked way, he shall die in his iniquity; but thou hast delivered thy soul** (Ezekiel 3:17–19). Ezekiel kept warning the people saying, *Thus saith the Lord, thus saith the Lord.*

God wants for His message to be the greatest encouragement to you. You may think He is hard, but

He is giving you a love-shaking to make Himself and His love a greater reality to you. He wants you to know how much you mean to Him and how much He's depending on you as a believer. Many in darkness have never had a chance like you have. Millions have never even had a Bible, never held the Word of God in their hands much less in their hearts; and we must take the message to them.

CHAPTER 6

Flesh And The Devil

What are the works of the flesh? In the fifth chapter of Galatians, the Lord, through the apostle Paul, lists seventeen of them. **Now the works of the flesh are manifest, which are these; Adultery, fornication, uncleanness, lasciviousness, Idolatry, witchcraft, hatred, variance, emulations, wrath, strife, seditions, heresies, Envyings, murders, drunkenness, revellings, and such like: of the which I tell you before, as I have also told you in time past, that they which do such things shall not inherit the kingdom of God** (Galatians 5:19–21). The words *such things* imply that there are even more than seventeen works, and we know there are many more according to the Word of God. However, this list narrows down the works of the flesh and gives people some idea of what the Lord will not allow into His heaven. Does this sound like the soul that sinneth shall die?—Absolutely! It sounds exactly like that.

Many people have never understood the seventeen works of the flesh, so I'm going to give you some definitions.

ADULTERY

Adultery, the first work of the flesh, refers to a married person having sexual intercourse outside of his or her own marriage. One cannot walk in the flesh, fulfilling the lust of the flesh, and walk in the Spirit, too. I say again, it's one way or the other.

FORNICATION

Fornication is any unlawful sexual intercourse, and this includes shacking-up and common-law marriages. The Lord said if you take pleasure in sin, you have no part in His Kingdom. Having intercourse without first being joined together by God is a sin. **What therefore God hath joined together, let not man put asunder** (Mark 10:9).

God is the one who planned sex, but the devil and man are deceiving a lot of people about it today. People living in sin are treated as though they are married. On special days they all mix together. What do the little children think? They know when people are not married; they know when they're sleeping together. Are you giving children a good example, teaching them the right way?

Preacher, are you talking to me?

If you're guilty, I am. If I had a son who was shacked-up, he wouldn't bring the girl to my house. I'd say, "Until you get married you'll have to come here alone. You're not sleeping together here. I don't endorse what you're doing; it's whoredom." Living with a common-law partner is just plain fornication no matter what anyone tells you.

This society is deceiving many already; if you're giving over a little bit to that deceit, you're being contaminated. I once read a letter on my telecast from a woman whose brother had been living with his girlfriend for a whole year. Then they planned a big wedding, white wedding gown and all. The family of the woman who had written was angry with her because she didn't go to the wedding or the reception. If I had a family like that I'd praise God for every day they didn't speak to me or call me! If they started criticizing my decision, I'd say, *Wrong number!* and cut them off.

God gave you a mouth and a backbone; and, if you use both in the right way, you'll please the Lord.

God is giving me this for you; it's really something to think about. You can't endorse everything. Some of you have come to the place that you don't think anything about unmarried people having sex. Even kids that go to church every Sunday have been so brainwashed by the devil that they think having sex is no different than kissing. I've dealt with them. They have no conscience, and they'll go to hell for it.

UNCLEANNESS

Anything in your life that's filthy, vile, obscene or morally impure is uncleanness. Uncleanness is seen much today, even among "Christians." Anyone with uncleanness in his or her life does not have the presence or the holiness of God. Unless there is a change, that one will lose his soul. The need for staying clean should be impressed upon your sons and daughters.

Today people laugh about someone being a virgin, but to be unclean before God is a fearful thing. God help us to stand holy in His presence, to know what we are in His eyes! Your home is your castle; what do you allow in it? You're responsible for whatever goes on in your home, responsible for the music and the actions. That's your home; and you, Mom and Pop, are the head of it.

LASCIVIOUSNESS

Expressing lust, tending to excite lustful desires is lascivious, and there's much of it today. People dress to tantalize others and show their nudity. I've seen it even in church, and it's a disgrace. Some girls don't hide much of their nakedness when they stand up, and it's a plain disgrace when they sit down.

Teach your children to dress right. Girls flaunting themselves is a degraded spirit that's raging. Those who are consecrated to God don't show their nakedness to tantalize others, to draw the opposite sex to them. Keep in mind that the kind of person you draw that way is the kind you're going to marry; and, all too often, it's a bad marriage.

Using your body to stir desire in another and to entice is lascivious behavior; God is displeased with that. Holy people do not flaunt themselves in lasciviousness and don't lead others into it.

IDOLATRY

What is idolatry? Excessive devotion to some person or thing; not putting God first is idolatry, for that means you have someone or something ahead of God. Jesus said, **Thou shalt love the Lord thy God with all thy heart, and with all thy soul, and with all thy mind** (Matthew 22:37).

Israel, remember, lost three thousand lives by making a golden calf to worship. **And the LORD said unto Moses, Go, get thee down; for thy people, which thou broughtest out of the land of Egypt, have corrupted themselves: They have turned aside quickly out of the way which I commanded them: they have made them a molten calf, and have worshipped it, and have sacrificed thereunto, and said, These be thy gods, O Israel, which have brought thee up out of the land of Egypt. And it came to pass, as soon as he came nigh unto the camp, that he saw the calf, and the dancing: and Moses' anger waxed hot, and he cast the tables** [the Ten Commandments] **out of his hands, and brake them beneath the mount. And he took the calf which they had made, and burnt it in the fire, and ground it to powder, and strawed it upon the water, and made the children of Israel drink of it . . . and there fell of the people that day about three thousand men** (Exodus 32:7,8,19,20,28). The Lord intended us to love and worship only Him with our whole being.

WITCHCRAFT

Witchcraft includes astrology, black magic, sorcery, giving over to or having supernatural powers of the devil through contact with evil spirits. God's people never use this kind of wickedness, these powers of the devil. Daniel didn't use any of it in Babylon.

Witches were burned under the Law. One of King Saul's transgressions, remember, was seeking out a witch. God let the devil take Saul over, and Saul eventually committed suicide. **So Saul died for his transgression which he committed against the LORD, even against the word of the LORD, which he kept not, and also for asking counsel of one that had a familiar spirit** [a witch]**, to inquire of it** (I Chronicles 10:13).

Are you taking part in any of these things? Do you allow the astrology columns to influence you in any way? Do you read what astrologers have to say? If so, you're playing with the devil. All aspects of the occult are works of the flesh, works of Lucifer. If Eve hadn't played with the devil she wouldn't have lost everything.

King Belshazzar called for the astrologers and soothsayers when the hand began to write on the wall. But the message was directly from God, and the devil didn't have the interpretation. **In the same hour came forth fingers of a man's hand, and wrote over against the candlestick upon the plaster of the wall of the king's palace: and the king saw the part of the hand that wrote. Then the king's countenance was changed, and his**

thoughts troubled him, so that the joints of his loins were loosed, and his knees smote one against another. The king cried aloud to bring in the astrologers, the Chaldeans, and the soothsayers. And the king spake, and said to the wise men of Babylon, Whosoever shall read this writing, and shew me the interpretation thereof, shall be clothed with scarlet, and have a chain of gold about his neck, and shall be the third ruler in the kingdom. Then came in all the king's wise men: but they could not read the writing, nor make known to the king the interpretation thereof (Daniel 5:5–8).

America is walking the same paths that Babylon walked. The price was death then, and the price is the same today. The hand that wrote the Ten Commandments for Moses is about to write again; this time it will include the destiny of our civilization. If you want to know your future, look into the Bible. This endtime hour is clearly laid out for all to see.

HATRED

Another work of the flesh is hatred, strong dislike of another person. Some of you toy with it and don't forgive people the way you should or as fast as you should. When you use Jesus' forgiveness instead of your own forgiveness, you will have no problem forgiving people of whatever they do against you. Why waste your time worrying about not forgiving someone? Turn your enemies over to God and trust your friends in the hands of God. Turning your enemies over to the left hand of God is the only and best place to put them.

If you have a strong dislike for another human being, you must pray and ask God to help you to ensure that no hatred is in your heart. Do you dislike or despise someone in a great way? Watch out! If that person is as bad as you think he or she is, that one is soon going to be in hell; and, if you have the same spirit, you'll be there, too. You don't have to like everyone—even God doesn't like everyone—but you must have God's love for his or her soul.

VARIANCE

Disagreement, disputing, quarrelling . . . there is much variance in homes today, much division. When both husband and wife are true children of God, the Lord will give them divine love to use so there will be great love between them.

Do you have any variance in your home that affects your children? If so it may well destroy them. However, in a praying home—a home with a family altar, one of love where sin is called sin—the children have every advantage. Not practicing sin, they learn to live in righteousness and holiness, and they learn to serve God's love.

Do you fuss in your home, disagree, and quarrel with those around you? Variance breaks up many marriages. Young people get married and then fuss and carry on, insisting on having their own way. Selfish and resentful, they can't get along. That isn't what God planned in marriage; it's of the flesh. They drive the presence of God away with their bickering. The Lord wants everyone to live in the cloud of His presence and not to drive His presence out of their home.

All couples do not fuss. If you're a fussing couple, pray that God will teach you how to change and love each other. Would you continue to argue if Jesus walked in? Some people do not know how to love anyone else but themselves. Learn how to love each other as the Lord wants you both to be loved.

The devil tells you it's healthy to fuss. Psychiatrists and psychologists claim the same thing because it's so wonderful to make up. That's the devil's thinking, snake-talk, and much of that talk goes on in our nation now as well as all over the world. If you profess to be a Christian, how do you think God looks upon actions that make Him appear so far away, small and insignificant? How do you think that makes Him feel? It's an insult to the Holy Spirit. The Spirit of

God does not nourish a disagreeable spirit; it is not the love of God nor the works of the Holy Spirit.

EMULATIONS

Emulations include envy, trying to compete because you're resentful of someone else, wanting to get the best of another, jealousy. As children of God you're part of the body of Christ; there is to be no jealousy or emulation among the body. The left hand was not made to dislike or try to overcome the right. The left eye is not supposed to become upset with the right and pout, sulk, and refuse to work. That pouting spirit is of the devil. How can you expect to keep the Holy Spirit and have a pouting devil in you?

Paul used physical bodies to describe the body of Christ. **For as the body is one, and hath many members, and all the members of that one body, being many, are one body: so also is Christ. For by one Spirit are we all baptized into one body, whether we be Jews or Gentiles, whether we be bond or free; and have been all made to drink into one Spirit. For the body is not one member, but many. If the foot shall say, Because I am not the hand, I am not of the body; is it therefore not of the body? And if the ear shall say, Because I am not the eye, I am not of the body; is it therefore** not of the body? If the whole body were an eye, where were the hearing? If the whole were hearing, where were the smelling? But now hath God set the members every one of them in the body, as it hath pleased him** (I Corinthians 12:12–18).

We all have our place in the body of Christ, and we all must be in harmony with the Spirit of God. No part of the human body criticizes any other part, and that's the way it's supposed to be in the body of Christ. If you think you cannot be free of emulations, if you allow them to be present in your life, the Lord will one day be free of you; and that's according to the teaching of the Word of God.

WRATH

A wrathful person has intense anger, vengeance, and carries out punishment in a great fit of rage and fury.

Are you vengeful? The Lord said, **Dearly beloved, avenge not yourselves, but rather give place unto wrath: for it is written, Vengeance is mine; I will repay, saith the Lord** (Romans 12:19). The Lord is the one to carry that spirit of vengeance. God let you know about His left hand of judgment and has shown you the works of His left hand, but we're supposed to be in His right hand all the time. The spirit in which He deals with His loving children is in the right hand. He never wants to serve one of us from the left hand. If He has to, He will; but, oh, how it hurts Him!

If someone slights you, are you without rest until you even the score? That's not the Spirit of God. Do you feel you have to even the score at your job? Years ago a man worked for me who had that spirit to even the score. If a person acted in a way he didn't like, he'd hide something the person needed to do their work for God.

"You can't act like that! It hinders the work of God, and God isn't pleased," I told him.

"Well, they were wrong," he would justify himself.

"It doesn't matter what they did. What you hid away and wouldn't let them find for days has hindered God's work; those tools belong to God."

The man had that ugly spirit of vengeance.

You'll never see these spirits or any of their works in heaven. The Lord is trying to free us from all of the works of the flesh, from any taint of them. The works of the flesh are more dangerous than dynamite or the H-bomb. Again, it's the right hand seeking to damage the left—how ridiculous!

The Lord told us to love our enemies, so imagine how much more we should love our friends, our brothers and sisters in Christ. **But I say unto you,**

Love your enemies, bless them that curse you, do good to them that hate you, and pray for them which despitefully use you, and persecute you; That ye may be the children of your Father which is in heaven (Matthew 5:44,45). The Bible has strong words for those who hate.

The works of the flesh aren't being taught the way they should be. Instead, people are being taught that they can't live free from sin; it's the devil's message, the same message he used to get over the walls of Eden.

Again in Luke we read, **Bless them that curse you, and pray for them which despitefully use you** (Luke 6:28). Jesus came to earth and showed us this could be done.

How can people be on their way to heaven when they're seeking vengeance against another child of God, telling unsavory stories about their shortcomings and mistakes? But some do that. Visitors have come to church who know nothing about anyone's past, and some members have brought up unpleasant things that happened to others years ago. That's disgraceful! God holds you responsible when you kill another's influence. If you'll search your spirit, you'll find something in your heart against that person, something contaminated that's spewing out of you. You won't try to run someone down whom you

Chapter 6:   Flesh And The Devil

love with all of your heart.

Whispering slimy tales about another is disgusting to God and disgusting to those who are right. How can you tear people down and still claim to have the love of God in your heart? Notice, I said *claim* to have the love of God. Tearing others down is a manifestation of the works of the flesh; the Spirit of God has nothing to do with it. If someone has wronged you, put him or her into the hands of God and pray for the person. Don't gossip about the person; let God handle it.

What if the Lord were to come at the exact moment you were getting revenge on someone? It's the same with fussing in your home. What if you're in the midst of a big fuss when the Rapture takes place? You'll be left here for the Tribulation Period, and that will be sad. When you fuss it's because you're drifting away from God. When you do any of these works of the flesh—even if you're contaminated just a little bit—you're drifting, and one of these days you'll be too far from the shore to get back.

If the Lord would pay you back for everything you've done to Him, there would be nothing left of you. Have you ever thought of that? It's easy for me to forgive people of whatever they do because one day the Lord forgave me of all my sins. He cast them away from Him to never mention them to me again; and, if you are saved, He did the same thing for you. **And their sins and iniquities will I remember no more** (Hebrews 10:17).

This is all the forgiveness you have, no more, no less: **And when ye stand praying, forgive, if ye have aught against any: that your Father also which is in heaven may forgive you your trespasses. But if ye do not forgive, neither will your Father which is in heaven forgive your trespasses** (Mark 11:25,26). Measure the forgiveness you can expect to receive by the amount you give to others, and that should help you. If you don't forgive others, you don't have the Spirit of the Lord.

But ye are not in the flesh, but in the Spirit, if so be that the Spirit of God dwell in you. Now if any man have not the Spirit of Christ, he is none of his (Romans 8:9). The Spirit of Jesus includes the spirit of forgiveness. If Jesus could be separated from forgiveness, we would have no salvation; we'd be men and women without hope, lost in sin.

You're either going to take on the Spirit of God or the spirit of the devil; you can't be in-between. Jesus said, **I am come a light into the world, that whosoever believeth on me should not abide in darkness** (John 12:46). The light of God penetrates the darkness of the devil, and we can't have that light if we continue to sin.

STRIFE

Contention with another is strife. It's conflict, not getting along with your brothers and sisters in Christ, making every day a battlefield. Some people never have any trouble with their brothers and sisters in the church, but others cause trouble.

It's been said that to keep a friend, never let that one borrow money; suggest that your friend use the bank. On the other hand, some of you have made enemies by borrowing money and not paying it back; maybe the debt has been neglected for years. Do you think you're going to heaven like that? That's dishonesty, a work of the flesh and not the work of the Holy Spirit.

If you're honest-hearted, you don't dodge people to whom you owe money; you'll do your best to pay back on the loan as often as you can, and I don't mean once a year either. Some of you tell me you're going to pay back what you've borrowed, and then you still don't pay. Is that the truth or is it a lie? The Holy Spirit is the Spirit of truth; you must abide by your word.

Minding other people's business is another work of the flesh that causes strife. People who have no business of their own tend to meddle in someone else's business.

Tattlers ... busybodies, speaking things which

they ought not (I Timothy 5:13): God detests these works of the flesh. Saying things you have no business saying causes strife in others, stirs up people to fight. Some of you keep your mouth open sixteen times bigger than it ought to be. When your brain and mouth don't work together, hurtful things fly out of your mouth; and, before you know it, you're a troublemaker. What you need is true salvation. When you are truly born again, you have a good, clean mouth the size Jesus had, **who did no sin, neither was guile found in his mouth** (I Peter 2:22).

Jesus took on the fashion of a man; He came under subjection to everything outside of Eden just as we have. Jesus showed us how to live free from sin. He brought the remedy: divine blood. Jesus, born of the Virgin Mary, had divine blood, life for all who will accept it, and accept it we must. What causes people to reject the blood and move away from the presence of God?—These works of the flesh that I'm talking about.

SEDITIONS

Rebellion, stirring up discontent, trying to enlist others into a conflict over some cause—real or imagined—are all forms of sedition. Today in America the so-called Christian world always has a cause of its own but not a real cause of the Lord. They're out marching and protesting, and they'll still be marching after the Rapture takes place.

Do you have a feeling of worth only when you're overreacting? People protest in the streets and even become violent in promoting some social cause in the name of religion. That's not Bible. Those people are not saved; they don't have an ounce of God. Deceived by the devil, they think they're doing a great work for God. They're doing nothing for God; they're a hurt to the cause of Christ. Winning souls for the Lord is what matters.

Are you critical? How do you use your tongue, with sweetness or vinegar? I heard a preacher say that he would give five thousand dollars to have a certain sermon back. It's been over fifty years ago that I heard that, and five thousand dollars then is more like a million today. I've never preached a sermon I'd give a nickel to get back. One thing people say when they listen to my tapes from years ago: *He preaches now just like he used to preach.* How else would I preach? The Gospel hasn't changed.

Do you cause division among the children of God? God may still love you, but He certainly doesn't like what you're doing. It's dangerous to be disliked by the Lord. You are in the flesh if you cause any disharmony in the body of Christ, for this is not the kind of conflict that comes by taking a stand for the whole Word of God, but the kind that comes from nitpicking, sowing seeds of bitterness, and sustaining turmoil. Whatever drives the presence of God from you will cause you to miss the Rapture. The Lord is warning you who are indulging in the works of the flesh that He will leave you behind when He comes.

It's time to clean up so the love of God can take you over. The Holy Spirit is available to all, but some resist Him. Self-centered, self-satisfied, they have let the enemy deceive them into thinking they're all right. That's the reason some talk too much and say things they have no business saying. Their opinions are worthless, and I hope everyone will recognize those opinions to be just that. Look out for people who are opinionated; stay away from them and turn to the Lord.

HERESIES

Teaching anything in opposition to the Word of God is heresy. Do you oppose any of the teachings of God's Word? Do you prefer man's doctrine to the truth of the Word? Check everything you hear about the Lord with the Word of God. The Word is your faith, your safety. **Beloved, believe not every spirit, but try the spirits whether they are of God: because many false prophets are gone out into the**

world (I John 4:1). Try the spirits with the Word.

Do you think the Holy Ghost baptism isn't necessary for you? Check the Word of God thoroughly with an open mind and find out what it says about the Holy Spirit. The Bible plainly states you must have the Holy Ghost baptism to make the Rapture, and to deny this fact is heresy. Man cannot deny what *thus saith the Lord* and expect to get by. The Bible says, **Let God be true, but every man a liar** (Romans 3:4). It doesn't matter how many preachers claim that you do not need the Holy Ghost to make the Rapture; all that matters is what the Word of God says. His Word stands whether people believe it or not. God spoke the Word, and He will not change it for anyone. **For I am the LORD, I change not** (Malachi 3:6).

It's a command for God's people to receive the Holy Ghost; **And, being assembled together with them, [Jesus] commanded them that they should not depart from Jerusalem, but wait for the promise of the Father, which, saith he, ye have heard of me. For John truly baptized with water; but ye shall be baptized with the Holy Ghost not many days hence** (Acts 1:4,5). The obedient will receive the Holy Ghost. **And we are his witnesses of these things; and so is also the Holy Ghost, whom God hath given to them that obey him** (Acts 5:32). God is not coming after the disobedient. No disobedience will be going up in the Rapture.

Do you believe in talking in tongues at will? Talking in tongues at will is heresy! Do you believe once in grace always in grace and yet you are sinning? It's heresy! After you receive salvation, I say again, you're in grace only as long as you do not commit willful sin. Sin will always take you from the grace of God. Do you believe you can be free from sin? That's not heresy; that's the truth. Those who say no one can be free from sin are calling God a liar.

Be careful with your life, with what kind of movies you see, with the places you go. Most movies made today are not fit for anything but your pets to watch, and those movies are liable to even affect them.

This is straight talk. I'm dealing with the works of the devil. Did you think it was going to be pleasant?

For a Christian to go to questionable places is dangerous. Today, even the sports world is full of gambling and cursing. You can hear people blaspheming God's name all around you, and free-for-all fights break out on the playing field and in the stands. If you take your children to those kinds of events, you could put their lives in jeopardy as well as your own. But the devil can keep easing you on into more and more things that take you away from

God if you'll let him.

But, Preacher, I don't take part in any of that.

You don't have to take part; you're automatically a part if you're there. You've joined with them and all that's going on. They fight among themselves—and who wants to watch those with so much devil in them that they're liable to blow up any minute? Even the police have to come in to separate people fighting among themselves, and that's not good. I don't like to be around people who blow up. Jesus said, **Peace I leave with you, my peace I give unto you: not as the world giveth, give I unto you. Let not your heart be troubled, neither let it be afraid** (John 14:27). Do you want to be around strife? Do you want to tune in to programs where people fight and carry on?

Some people think it's all right to go to a casino and indulge in gambling. You wouldn't catch me dead in a place like that. Yet some so-called Christians will board a plane and off they go to that kind of entertainment.

Do you know what makes you a child of God? The divine blood. When you take the blood where it shouldn't go, you're dishonoring the blood. If you go to the wrong places, you're not a user of the blood.

But, Preacher, I'm going to use the blood and be

a winner.

You had better say you're going to be a winner for the Lord. What would children of God think if they happened to drive by and see you in a place you know God wouldn't approve of? How could they ever have any confidence in you? I wouldn't have any confidence in you; your testimony would have no effect on me. I would assume you're not a child of God. As a sinner I knew better than to gamble. I knew what children of God were like before I ever became born again because I watched them.

As a child, people affected me for good or bad, and I was hurt if someone in our church backslid. For example, there was a talented young singer in the church; I loved to hear her sing. She played the guitar and sang for the glory of God; her song had a wonderful message in it:

I'll tell you a story of the sanctified life.
It's a life set apart from all sin.

She was full of the Holy Ghost, full of the presence of God—then she backslid. I was ten or eleven years old at the time; and, when I heard she had gone away from God, I was crushed. But years later in Charlotte, North Carolina, she and her husband came to one of my services, and I learned that she had come back to the Lord and was teaching Sunday school at her church. Her husband was baptized in the Holy Ghost that Sunday afternoon. However, it brings sadness to me yet today when I think about what a shock it was when, as a child, I heard she had turned her back on the Lord.

We must be careful with our lives in this final hour, careful of the places we go. We can't go to the things of the world, can't take part in the fights, the races, the betting, and the cursing. You could be killed suddenly, and that wouldn't be a good testimony.

There are places you just can't go to because they're full of the all-out spirit of Antichrist. Sports were very different when I was a child. I never heard of fighting during the games, never dreamed of such things happening. They didn't allow us to fight in school, and we didn't fight in the small games. Do you see the difference? We're almost to the end now, and *you have the chance to separate or be left, saith the Lord.*

ENVYING

When you have feelings of ill will and discontent because of another's advantages, possessions, and blessings, you are envying. Do you resent anyone? If so, do you also resent God, the God who blessed another brother or sister in Christ Jesus with something you think you should have? The Lord teaches against envying anyone, those in Christ and those in the world.

If you're born again, be thankful first of all that you're God's child. You're rich, a millionaire, if you know God today. You may envy the wealth of a worldly person, but would you take his or her place on tomorrow when ill health or death comes?

Jesus told of a certain rich man who fared sumptuously every day and had everything anyone could want. Then there was Lazarus, a poor beggar who was sick, weak, and full of sores and who asked for just the crumbs; he was as low as the dogs. The rich man wanted nothing to do with the beggar. **And it came to pass, that the beggar died, and was carried by the angels into Abraham's bosom: the rich man also died, and was buried; And in hell he lift up his eyes, being in torments, and seeth Abraham afar off, and Lazarus in his bosom. And he cried and said, Father Abraham, have mercy on me, and send Lazarus, that he may dip the tip of his finger in water, and cool my tongue; for I am tormented in this flame. But Abraham said, Son, remember that thou in thy lifetime receivedst thy good things, and likewise Lazarus evil things: but now he is comforted, and thou art tormented. And beside all this, between us and you there is a great gulf fixed: so that they which would pass from hence to you cannot; neither can they pass to us,**

that would come from thence. Then he [the rich man] **said, I pray thee therefore, father, that thou wouldest send him to my father's house: For I have five brethren; that he may testify unto them, lest they also come into this place of torment. Abraham saith unto him, They have Moses and the prophets; let them hear them. And he said, Nay, father Abraham: but if one went unto them from the dead, they will repent. And he said unto him, If they hear not Moses and the prophets, neither will they be persuaded, though one rose from the dead** (Luke 16:22–31).

Many were envied while they were alive; but today they're in hell, and their possessions are useless to them. They are now paupers and will be for a trillion years and more.

TRUST GOD AND HONOR HIM!

Walk with God. He will bless you and look out for you as long as you put your whole trust in Him and are free from the works of the flesh. God did not promise to supply all your wants but rather to supply all your needs. He has promised heaven to believers, and with heaven comes all that anyone's heart could ever long for and more. **But as it is written, Eye hath not seen, nor ear heard, neither have entered into the heart of man, the things** which God hath prepared for them that love him (I Corinthians 2:9). In eternity, wonders beyond the imagination are promised to those who separate from the works of the flesh.

God tried giving man all that his heart desired on earth, but it didn't work. When times were good, many forgot about God. But in hard times they looked to God, cared about Him, felt the need of Him.

The Israelites spoiled the Egyptians and began their journey to freedom with great riches; they were blessed as they left Egypt. However, they took the gold from those riches and made a golden calf. Their actions destroyed much.

What is your god today? Who is your god? Is the Almighty God your God, or have you lost your first love? Do you look to the entertainment of the world to keep you going? Take a lesson from Israel in the wilderness, and be careful to use what God gives you wisely for His honor and glory.

Let your conversation be without covetousness; and be content with such things as ye have: for he hath said, I will never leave thee, nor forsake thee (Hebrews 13:5). God promised to never leave you nor forsake you; but, when you take yourself out of the presence of God, God's hands are tied.

To walk in the Spirit means you're not touched by

envy but are thanking and praising God, ready to meet Jesus at any time. When you're a new creation in Christ Jesus, you have much to be thankful for!

MURDERERS

Willfully killing yourself or another human being is murder. Not much value is put on human life today; little children haven't been taught to value human life.

Justice is not always rendered when someone commits murder. Those without God may not hand down a just verdict, letting people go free who shouldn't go free and putting a great penalty on those who need sympathy and help. People who don't live for God don't have the mind of God. Anyone who is going to judge others should have the mind of God.

Some of the decisions being made today are worthless at best. The need for discipline seems obscure to many people. Murderers and rapists are paroled, and they commit the same crimes all over again. Why? The devilish, demon-possessed soul that led to murder or rape in the first place has not been dealt with or delivered. We live in an hour that has more people walking in the flesh than are walking in the Spirit.

DRUNKENNESS

Liquor flows freely today, and demons can easily take over minds given in abandonment to alcohol.

One alcoholic asked me how he became devil possessed, and the Lord immediately told me. When he was drunk, the devils took him over.

People on drugs have many devils in them; drugs take over the brain faster than alcohol. It's dreadful how drugs paralyze the brain. All kinds of intoxicants are sold and readily available to all, even children. Drugs are obtained undercover in our schools; even children pedal drugs. There's a price to pay when people go the way of the flesh; we live in a flesh world.

Every kingdom in the past that has gone the way of the flesh has been destroyed. The Roman Kingdom, the Babylonian Kingdom and others down through history were destroyed. It's no different today. This is an age of intoxication. In order to be hospitable, people offer drinks and can easily be offended if the alcohol is refused. Anything to escape reality is common today. People not able to handle their self-image or the life they're living try to alter that image the wrong way and attempt to escape through alcohol and drugs. It's drugs and alcohol they need to escape from, and they can do it through the blood of Jesus. Our only hope is through the Lord.

Chapter 6: Flesh And The Devil

If you are a new creation in Christ Jesus, yield all to Him every day. Avoid the works of the flesh, and He will make you what you should be. Only when you take on the mind of Christ can you get along with yourself and think the way He thinks. Evaluate things by God's standards, and then you will have God's opinions, His thoughts and not yours.

REVELING

Revelings go on all around us with people delighting in wild parties and boisterous good times. Through television and the Internet, reveling can be brought right into your home. There's no need to complain about what's on the airways if you regularly watch.

Well, I just want to see what's on.

The devil certainly can be deceiving! Some people get on the Internet to see nudity and to watch people having intercourse. It's none of your business what's on the Internet if it's not God's business. Your business is holiness, righteousness, and eternal life. Your business is getting people saved, not indulging in revelings. If you turn on porn, you might as well face the fact that you're looking at it for your own gratification. Pornography is raging, and much devil possession comes with it. Like alcohol and drugs, it will intoxicate; but you can be delivered from it through the blood.

As an illustration, Webster gives this definition of reveling: *He revels in sports.* People certainly revel in sports today. Of course it's not a sin to kick or hit a ball; but, when you make sports your god, you're in trouble. What kind of crowds do you go into? If just about everyone around you is lost, that's no fellowship. How close to God do you feel later?

People want the presence and favor of God, but they want it when they want it. In many homes, sports is god on Sunday and every other day of the week; and, if people are not watching games, they're talking about them. In the work world, you notice that sports are the first thing people usually talk about on Monday mornings.

The Monday morning after I got saved, I talked about Jesus; I had something marvelous to talk about. I was young, in my teens, and still lit up from the night before when I passed a woman who exclaimed, "Oh, you look happy!"

"I am happy," I said, "and I'll be back to tell you about it."

I was on the way to do something else. When I finished and came back, I told her how I had been blessed in the service the night before. She just looked at me, but she had already confessed I looked happy; she couldn't deny that. We had had a great time at church the previous night and my soul-cup had run over, filling up the saucer and more. I went to church to get filled up with all the goodness and power of God I could.

Young people, if you're hooked on something destructive, get rid of it. Is it more important to you than God? Do you ever miss the anointed church services because you want to go to events in the world? If so, you're in trouble and in danger of running away from God completely. When you no longer take time for the work of God and you miss a service for any kind of sports or anything else that isn't necessary, you are lukewarm at best. If lingering in God's presence doesn't mean that much to you, if you no longer take time with God, He will be driven away from you by your own indifference.

Once again, these are the seventeen works of the flesh: adultery, fornication, uncleanness, lasciviousness, idolatry, witchcraft, hatred, variance, emulations, wrath, strife, seditions, heresies, envyings, murders, drunkenness, revelings. But the devil has many more works; are you free from all of them? Identifying the works of the flesh and checking to see if any of them are in your life is a good measuring rod, better than you realize. Never try to justify your actions with regard to the works of the flesh or you'll find yourself in that place where all flesh-works will be cast one day—the lake of fire.

The works of the flesh are the most dangerous bombs around us, the most dangerous of all diseases. They're more dangerous than cancer, tuberculosis, heart trouble, paralysis, AIDS or the AIDS virus, more dangerous than physical death itself. Some people are terrified of certain diseases, but they're not afraid of the works of the flesh. How sad indeed!

DON'T COMPROMISE

It's time to wake up and see the things that are coming upon the earth. Our hearts are not going to fail us; we're not going to run for cover and live in fear. We're going to take this Gospel to the whole world; it's a must. Daniel didn't consider the danger he was in by praying to God and not to the king. The three Hebrew boys didn't consider the danger they were in when they withstood the king's command to worship an idol. It didn't matter to them; they were ready to give their lives.

All members of the bridal company must come to the place they would give their lives before they would compromise the will of God. You're not going to win members of your family by compromising with them. Some of you have hurt your testimony by compromising, by allowing wrong things to come into your home or be in your home, associating with what you know is wrong. What if the earth would open in your presence to swallow up those whom you are endorsing by letting them come into your home? You'd be swallowed up, too.

Do you compromise with your children? If you're not careful, you can let the devil rob you of your soul, of eternal life. One day in hell, in the lake of fire, you'll lift up your eyes all because you compromised with your children and let them bring sin into your home; you endorsed it, gave over to it.

But, Preacher, everyone does it nowadays.

No, everyone doesn't do it. Those who live in the works of the flesh do it, but those who live in the Spirit don't.

God wants you to examine yourself today, examine your home. What do you allow in your home? What kind of literature or magazines do you have there? What do you allow your grown children to bring into your home? Don't compromise with family, friends, or enemies; just live by the Word of God. That's what you're supposed to do. It's time to decide to separate from everything of the world; the hour is so late. Come out of this world before it's destroyed. There's only one flight out; and, if you miss it, you could scream your lungs out, *Come back! Don't leave me!*—but you'd still be left.

I love you too much to not give you the truth. If I didn't love you, I'd just give you a pat on the back and say, *I know you'll be all right; God wouldn't send you to hell.* But your sins will send you to hell, and you might as well face it. These are the things you should be warning your children about—the works of the flesh.

CHAPTER 7

More Works Of The Flesh

The price for our salvation has been fully paid for us. All things needed to live free from sin are available, so the Lord has seen to it that many, many sins are listed throughout the New Testament.

Paul writing to the Romans gave them a big list of sins. Rome was an ungodly place; many Christians lost their lives there. They died in the arena, were fed to the lions, burned at the stake, tortured and killed in various ways. The Roman Kingdom was degraded, and the world is degraded today as well.

MORE WORKS OF THE FLESH LISTED

And even as they did not like to retain God in their knowledge, God gave them over to a reprobate mind, to do those things which are not convenient; Being filled with all unrighteousness, fornication, wickedness, covetousness, maliciousness; full of envy, murder, debate, deceit, malignity; whisperers, Backbiters, haters of God, despiteful, proud, boasters, inventors of evil things, disobedient to parents, Without understanding, covenantbreakers, without natural affection, implacable, unmerciful: Who knowing the judgment of God, that they which commit such things are worthy of death, not only do the same, but have pleasure in them that do them (Romans 1:28–32). If you commit the sins in this chapter, you're worthy of death. And, remember, if you take pleasure in sins that others are committing, you're just as worthy of death as they are.

A REPROBATE MIND

Continuing to identify the works of the flesh, I want you to consider the word *reprobate*. A reprobate mind is depraved and vicious; it's a mind rejected by God, excluded from salvation and lost in sin. A reprobate person has a mind that is condemned by God.

God looks on a person who has a reprobate mind as worthless, a person beyond saving. The people in Sodom and Gomorrah had reprobate minds beyond saving, and the Lord destroyed them. The civilization in Noah's day was beyond saving as well, and God destroyed them with a flood.

Reprobate also means foreordained to damnation by God even while the soul is still in the body. Many souls are foreordained now for eternal damnation; they have gone beyond saving and sinned against the Holy Ghost.

Men of corrupt minds, reprobate concerning the faith (II Timothy 3:8). These men have depraved, violent minds concerning the Gospel that Jesus brought; they have vicious minds. The Gospel either edifies and blesses you or it condemns you to eternal damnation. The Gospel is powerful to the righteous to deliver and powerful enough to the unrighteous to destroy.

In the Old Testament, the sin against the Holy Ghost was never mentioned, although some had committed it. Few people lived free from sin in Old Testament days. Today all who want to can live sin-free; Jesus came with the remedy; His blood made it possible.

Do you still think you can't live free from sin? Well, then the wrath of God is on you because the wrath of God will come against all sin and all ungodliness. By not living in the truth of God, you hold to unrighteousness. The only way to hold the truth is to love it and live it.

RESULTS OF THE REPROBATE MIND

Wherefore God also gave them up to uncleanness through the lusts of their own hearts, to dishonour their own bodies between themselves: Who changed the truth of God into a lie, and worshipped and served the creature more than the Creator, who is blessed forever. Amen. For this cause God gave them up unto vile affections: for even their women did change the natural use into that which is against nature: And likewise also the men, leaving the natural use of the woman, burned in their lust one toward another; men with men working that which is unseemly, and receiving in themselves that recompence of their error which was meet (Romans 1:24-27). This is where the terrible sin of homosexuality came in, and homosexuality is raging all over the world today. It's unbelievable to those with normal desires—men marrying men, women marrying women. In at least one state the same sex can now marry. Many such couples want to adopt and raise children in this ungodly atmosphere.

But in this final hour, homosexuals will be delivered more than ever before just as people are delivered from HIV/AIDS. Many have been delivered down through the years in this Jesus ministry, and there will be many, many more. Untold thousands of homosexuals want to be free.

What I call real homosexuals are those who are born that way. They have the body of one sex and the nature and desire of the other sex, and it has to be reversed in them to be made right. It's as simple for God to do that as it is for Him to breathe or to move a little finger.

The finger of God does many mighty things. The finger of God wrote the Ten Commandments, and those love fingers will deliver people who really want deliverance; but there's no hope for those who won't accept it. No matter how much homosexuality is endorsed, the practicing homosexual will not get into God's heaven. To enter heaven they must be redeemed, set free through the blood of the Lamb and no longer live the homosexual lifestyle.

In Sodom, the two angels who went to see Lot looked like men, and the men of the city thought they were men. **The men of the city, even the men of Sodom, compassed the house round, both old and young, all the people from every quarter: And they called unto Lot, and said unto him, Where are the men which came in to thee this night? bring them out unto us, that we may know them. And Lot went out at the door unto them, and shut**

the door after him, And said, I pray you, brethren, do not so wickedly. Behold now, I have two daughters which have not known man; let me, I pray you, bring them out unto you, and do ye to them as is good in your eyes: only unto these men do nothing; for therefore came they under the shadow of my roof. But the men put forth their hand, and pulled Lot into the house to them, and shut to the door. And they smote the men that were at the door of the house with blindness, both small and great: so that they wearied themselves to find the door (Genesis 19:4–8,10,11).

Some people have wondered why a father would offer his daughters. Lot knew what the men wanted, and he knew their desires: It was men with men. He lived in the midst of that people, saw all of the filth going on, and he said, *Don't do this great sin.*

The devil has deceived many who think homosexuality is all right. You see it on television more and more. Homosexuality is being brought forth, just like other sins of the past, until it is recognized in our society and accepted.

God is the only hope for the homosexual. God hates homosexuality, but He loves the homosexual. Those who don't want to admit it's sinful say that Jesus didn't say anything about homosexuality. But what Paul said was the same as Jesus saying it; his condemnation came from heaven. Homosexuals don't want to go into the Pauline epistles because their sin is all spelled out there, and it's in the Old Testament as well. But they want to take freedom, as they call it, through misusing the Word of God. It's an awful hour, and things are going to get worse.

The Lord will forgive people when they repent. He'll deliver them from any kind of lust and set them free, but those who continue to practice adultery and homosexuality will go to hell for it. Sin is sin, and the Lord is separating sin from righteousness.

God classified all sin as worthy of destruction. All kinds of sins were being committed in Noah's day and in Sodom and Gomorrah. Because people had degraded themselves beyond hope of deliverance, God destroyed them. Those civilizations didn't have the light of God's will.

Adam and Eve had failed to live sin-free and probably had not been careful to train their children the way they should, but the Lord had mercy on their descendants. Jesus offered salvation to those who lived in the days of Noah. Many people don't know this, but the Bible plainly tells us about it: While the body of Jesus was in the tomb, His Spirit preached to those who were in prison. This is not my thought; this is God's knowledge. **For Christ also hath once suffered for sins, the just for the unjust, that he**

might bring us to God, being put to death in the flesh, but quickened by the Spirit: By which also he went and preached unto the spirits in prison; Which sometime were disobedient, when once the longsuffering of God waited in the days of Noah, while the ark was a-preparing, wherein few, that is, eight souls were saved by water (I Peter 3:18–20).

A gulf once separated Paradise from hell. Jesus preached across that gulf; He became the bridge for those who had been disobedient while Noah was building the ark. That gulf had been there ever since God made a heaven for man to go to and a hell for the devil and his angels. Those in hell could see the ones who were at peace in heaven; however, those in heaven couldn't see the ones on the other side of the gulf. Jesus preached the Cross to those who had died in the Flood; and, for the first time, they had a bridge. What a blessed time it was!

Doesn't this tell you what grace will do? Only one family found grace in the eyes of God before the Flood; but, after the Crucifixion, the bridge went up and gave those people of Noah's day a chance at salvation. They had been in such ignorance of the will of God as well as of the Creator and the love of God. However, we have no record of others being given a second chance like that. Those people were given one chance and one chance only. Jesus brought the ones who accepted Him across the gulf; and, when He ascended, He took them to heaven, took their souls right on with Him. Isn't that wonderful!

MALIGNITY

Malignity is great malice, ill will and an intense desire to harm others. Today people throughout the world have an intense desire to destroy good people. The Lord let us know this kind of hatred would come, and it's here. Great malice, the quality of being very harmful, has made many people dangerous.

Plotting a secret confidence of hatred, hinting at something evil, or a rumor are all malignities. In this final hour, God's people, the Bride, will speak with love. She will have facts to back up what is necessary to talk about because she will be a speaker of the truth. The Bride will be truthful in all her ways and walk hand-in-hand with truth. She will embrace the truth that Jesus brought and taught.

IMPLACABLE

Not easily appeased or pacified, people are restless, implacable. Even many Christians are bothered with restlessness. The devil can make you so restless that you don't take time with God the way you ought to and don't enjoy fellowship with the Lord. You fail to be conscious of His love for you and His desire to fellowship with you, to walk and talk with you and let you know you're His very own.

Babies are given pacifiers to try to quiet them down, but there are a lot of Christians who need a pacifier they can't buy at the store; they can only get it through the Holy Spirit. Some Christians can't seem to spend any time at home with the Lord; they're on the move and never satisfied. On a rainy day they're walking the floor, depressed.

I love a shut-in day and love for my telephone to stop ringing. I love the early hours of two-three-four-or five o'clock in the morning. People don't usually call at those hours unless someone has died. Quiet time with the Lord is wonderful. The Lord has visited me much at night, and I love being alone with Him.

As your anointings become greater, the restlessness will settle down. Family or friends won't be around you all the time, and you won't feel the need to be out driving the streets or walking here and there. The more you take of these ultimate anointings, the more the Spirit will be able to be real to you. You will feel that tender touch from the Comforter that gives you comfort like a loving mother.

I can still see my mom laying a hand on the little

ones in the family and those little ones getting quiet. Mama's hand was different; the baby knew that hand. Maybe it had been fretting, crying, and one or two of us would try to do something with it, but we couldn't do anything. Then Mom would come in, lay a loving hand on that baby and whisper, "shush." That little one knew her voice like one dove knows the cooing of another dove, and the baby would drift off into sweet sleep.

That loving hand—you must have the loving hand of the Comforter with you, Child, all the time.

Daniel had insight into this restless age thousands of years ago. **But thou, O Daniel, shut up the words, and seal the book, even to the time of the end: many shall run to and fro, and knowledge shall be increased** (Daniel 12:4). Daniel was saying that, in the last days, many will be restless and dissatisfied. Jesus talked about Daniel; in the eyes of heaven he was a mighty prophet, one of the very greatest.

Don't take on the influence of this sin; don't be implacable. Let the Holy Spirit bring peace to you and appease your spirit so you can be quiet. The Psalmist said, **Be still, and know that I am God** (Psalm 46:10).

Although you don't sin, your spirit can be influenced and affected by the spirit of the devil through the spirit of sin that others have. As you battle sin, the going can get rough and you have to earnestly plead the blood, use the blood, because those demons of sin close in and get close to you. Although they're not in your soul, they still can affect you; but never forget that you have the blood to use. Don't let them influence you in any way; don't let them slow you down in your fasting life, in your prayer life, in your Bible life. Be ever learning and coming into more and more knowledge of the truth.

MALICIOUSNESS

Malice is an awful sin that some so-called Christians are tainted with; I run across it again and again. Just a tiny speck of malice in people will show up. They want to put someone else down, talk against that person; in fact, some delight in doing just that. If you have something critical to say, direct it to one of the trusted men of God and not to members of the church or even a member of your own family no matter who they are.

I didn't tell Angel everything I knew about people; she didn't need to battle against what they were going through. I wanted to protect her. There are things I know about some people I wouldn't want anyone else to know. But when the Lord washes the disobedience or sin away from them, it's gone as far as I'm concerned.

Some people delight in holding on to the mistakes of others; they'll talk about them, refer to them, and go back to dig up dirt in their lives that the blood has already washed away. Now they carry the scum of malice and are so much in need of fumigating that the Lord can't walk close to them. They're a stench in the nostrils of God. Make sure you aren't one who gives off such a foul odor!

The Lord is warning those on the fringes now. He's going on—with you or without you; you're not going to hold back this great, last worldwide revival. You can go on with Him or be left behind; you can go all the way and make the Rapture or lag behind and miss it. It's your choice.

Malice is that hateful spirit of doing things for spite. What if God would use such a spirit on you? Thank God He doesn't.

Maliciousness also means to be intentionally harmful. But when a preacher confronts some about their malicious words or actions, they let on as though they didn't mean anything hurtful; they claim they were just joking. If they had God in them, they wouldn't be joking to hurt people; and, when they were warned about it, they would shape up. Jesus said **that every idle word that men shall speak, they shall give account thereof in the day of judg-**

ment (Matthew 12:36). Since we have to give an account for every idle word, we had better keep our words in harmony with the Holy Spirit; then there will be nothing for which to give an account.

DEBATE AND DECEIT

Debate is fussing about the Gospel or anything else, arguing for the sake of argument.

Deceit has many forms. To understand it more fully, read my book *The Deceit of Lucifer* which is a thorough study on this subject.

WHISPERERS

If you whisper something undercover, especially if you know it's not right, your whisper is like the hissing of a serpent. Knowing you're telling something judgmental about another person condemns you before God.

Do you know what I heard? Now, I don't know for sure if it is true. . . . That means you don't have the truth in you; you're a whisperer! People whisper to get others thinking wrong about someone. They're plotting in secret confidence, hinting damaging thoughts about a person to usher you down the wrong path about them. They'll whisper a rumor to you when they have no facts to back it up just to make themselves feel important and powerful.

BACKBITERS

What is a backbiter? To speak maliciously about a person who is not present is backbiting. They have no chance to refute what you're saying. Do you know you can be sued for slander? Being sued is bad enough, but to go to hell for it and be cast into the lake of fire is even worse. All these works of the flesh, as well as every container contaminated with them, are going into the lake of fire, into the garbage dump for all sin. God help us to wake up! To be a backbiter is far below God; He never takes part in anything like that.

HATERS OF GOD

Many people hate God today; they may not admit it openly, but their actions show it. They don't want others to sing about Jesus Christ, the Son of God, nor do they want anything to do with Christmas—unless they can sell some non-religious holiday item and make a profit on it. Not wanting the Lord to be mentioned, they're going to a place where God won't want His name mentioned either. He will seal them off so He can't hear when His name is used in vain; that's how much God thinks of His name and the names of His Son, Jesus, and the Holy Spirit.

Haters of God, even so-called Christians and ministers, hate this Jesus outreach ministry. They hate the Holy Ghost; they say tongues are from the devil—but that's not what the Bible says. Many preachers have already sealed their doom by blaspheming against the Holy Spirit. They take their reprobate minds into pulpits they've made unholy. It's a disgrace what they're feeding the people; it's less than worthless straw.

DESPITEFUL

Oh, that old despiteful spirit is so destructive! The Lord told His people, **Fret not thyself because of evildoers, neither be thou envious against the workers of iniquity** (Psalm 37:1). God has already planned to give us rest from evildoers: **Come unto me, all ye that labour and are heavy laden, and I will give you rest. Take my yoke upon you, and learn of me; for I am meek and lowly in heart: and ye shall find rest unto your souls** (Matthew 11:28,29).

How long have you carried an enemy or enemies in your spirit who have taken your rest and made you a nervous wreck? I believe in putting my enemies under the blood, and then I go on my way with the burden for the lost—it's the only way to please God.

PROUD

It's strange how people can be so proud of who they are when they're a big nothing in the eyes of God; it's false pride. They won't look into God's mirror to see what they really look like; if they do, it's only for a moment and then they turn away and forget what manner of person they are. **For if any be a hearer of the word, and not a doer, he is like unto a man beholding his natural face in a glass: For he beholdeth himself, and goeth his way, and straightway forgetteth what manner of man he was** (James 1:23,24).

People will decide they're all right; they look as good as someone else they know. But that someone may be looking just like the devil in the eyes of God. The real question is: Do you look like Jesus? The Holy Spirit works with you so you can look and act just like Jesus, talk and pray like Him, so you can pray through the blood and get your prayers answered. *Father, you always hear me* is to be the thought of every son or daughter of God.

Many people are proud of how much money they make. Some even say, *This suit set me back so much that I've left the price tag on it.* Who cares? Have you met people like that?

A preacher in a high place in his organization was once telling me how expensive his suit was.

In those days I had never dreamed of being able to pay that much for a suit. But I had more victory in my soul wearing my cheap suit than he had in his soul wearing his expensive suit that he was boasting about. When you're full of God, worldly pride is repulsive to you.

BOASTERS

People try to impress others by boasting about what they have. They boast of evil, lift themselves up and think they're special in the world. They have the same boasting spirit the devil has. If you put them on God's scales, they wouldn't register. You can have fine possessions, but you don't have to brag about them. You could be a pauper tomorrow. The rich man that Jesus told us about had everything one moment, and the next moment he was in hell, a pauper.

When people are boasting to you, think of this scripture: **In my Father's house are many mansions: if it were not so, I would have told you. I go to prepare a place for you. And if I go and prepare a place for you, I will come again, and receive you unto myself; that where I am, there ye may be also** (John 14:2,3).

Boast about what God is doing, how He's helping us take Jesus to the world. Boast about the power, the greatness, and the love of God that He offers to all who accept Him.

Boasting about who you are, how much money you make and how much you have in the bank tells people that you've put your security in possessions and not in God.

God looks in on everyone and weighs every spirit separately. He can scan a crowd and know the condition of each person's soul. He knows if you smell like heaven or hell.

Why am I bringing you the hellish things of the devil? You must know about him so he cannot deceive you.

It's a separating time; the Lord wants His Bride to be holy **that he might present it to himself a glorious church, not having spot, or wrinkle, or any such thing; but that it should be holy and without blemish** (Ephesians 5:27). Be careful whom you run around with, whom you talk to; you may begin to smell just like they do.

INVENTORS OF EVIL THINGS

Do you know a person who is always inventing something evil to do? People come on television now to show just how evil they are. They delight in showing their bodies, delight in dirty talk, cursing, and giving every word a double meaning. I can't stand them. When they come across on TV, I can almost smell their stink! Telling all kinds of degraded stories on themselves, they think it's smart; it's the devil's idea of smart.

DISOBEDIENT TO PARENTS

You who have children are at war, for your children are exposed to the Antichrist's spirit of this age at almost every turn. Some of the ugliest kids who have ever walked this earth are here now, just as ugly and disobedient as the children were on the streets of Sodom and Gomorrah when the Lord destroyed them with fire and brimstone. They're as disobedient as the ones God drowned in Noah's day. God is about to bring worldwide judgment again.

Watch over your children; give them a lot of love and grace. Tell them what sin is and what righteousness is. Parents must feel the obligation to build character in their children. Character isn't something a person is born with; it has to be built within. The Psalmist says, **Behold, I was shapen in iniquity, and in sin did my mother conceive me** (Psalm 51:5). We were born the same way. Love has to be put into us; we aren't born with that love until we are born again.

Take time to build character in your children. In my family, we were taught to apologize when we were in the wrong, and that's embarrassing for a child; however, it was what I needed more times than one. I hated to apologize when I was a kid, but I had better look sorry when I said I was sorry or Mama wouldn't accept the apology. To tell my brother I was sorry was a definite chore. Standing up on the inside, I was just sorry I hadn't done more to him; but I couldn't tell Mama that.

My parents believed we should apologize if we talked impolitely to someone older. They didn't let us offend the neighbors; they taught us differently. You need to teach your children these things as well; they don't get away from those teachings.

Although my parents are in heaven, they keep reaching out to me daily with the godly things they told me, the wonderful examples they set for me. It was good for us to see our parents down on their knees before the Lord; every child had to keep quiet and honor God. We never thought about doing anything less. Children in our family learned at a young age to bow their heads at the table. *Keep those heads down until we thank the Lord and grace this food that we're about to eat because it's through His love that we have it.* That kind of teaching sticks with you.

I remember one time when Angel and I were traveling. We stopped at a diner along the highway. Our meal was served, and we bowed our heads in prayer.

No sooner had we said *Amen* than the excited owner rushed over to us.

"Oh, in all these years we've had this restaurant, you're the first people who have ever bowed their heads and thanked God for their food before they ate," she exclaimed.

We hadn't thought anything about it; it was just what we always did. Although we never met her again, I'm sure she remembered us. People are affected when they see the character of the Lord Jesus Christ in others.

My parents always gave us discipline with love. Rather than fussing with anyone who told them their children were misbehaving, they thanked the person for telling them; they wanted to know about it. We could deny it all we wanted to, but they had been told.

It's grievous to be disobedient to godly parents, and disobedience is more prevalent in these last days than in the past. The latter part of the sixties is when the moral decline began in earnest. The devils swarmed over America in a way they hadn't been able to before, and that's the reason we are where we are now, the reason so many children have committed suicide or been killed and destroyed for all eternity.

Remember the scripture: **Honour thy father and**

thy mother: that thy days may be long upon the land which the LORD thy God giveth thee (Exodus 20:12). That's a promise with a condition. To have long life, you must honor your godly parents. However, children can't honor sinful parents who want them to do things that God disapproves of.

This is a disobedient age. The Bible lets us know that the spirit of disobedience will work in the last days. Parents, take note of all your ways; make sure you have plenty of love and truth in the home, plenty of lasting peace, joy, and cooperation on your part. Take time for your children; listen to them. A child without a parent's good listening ear gets the wrong advice from other sources.

Parents are responsible for their children, responsible for every word they speak, responsible for where they go until they come to a certain age. Parents are supposed to serve love and understanding. It's tragic for a child to go to one of his or her parents and be told, *I'm too busy; go away. I don't have time for that now.* Your household may be a busy place, but never let it be too busy for a child who needs help or extra love and care. It means everything for children to know they are loved.

It isn't money that gives real security; it's love, truth, hope, courage and strength. Although the Lord has all of that for our children, it must be served by a human instrument because children can't see God, Jesus or the Holy Spirit.

Parents, make sure that when you have disagreements you don't have them in front of your children. Their little ears do not need to hear it; they do not need to shed tears over battling parents or hide behind the couch in fear that something terrible is about to happen. If there's anything children really need in the home, it's the love, peace and togetherness of a mother and father, knowing that parents agree.

It may have seemed cruel when you were a child and you asked your mother if you could do something, and she would want to know, "What did your father say?" I tried that more times than one, and I always hated that question. Why did they have to bring that up? But the things I used to hate, now I love; I found out they were good for me. At the time, however, I didn't want one parent to consider what the other parent thought; I just wanted to know if the first one I asked would let me do what I wanted, and then I could take off. It's good that I had the parents I had or I don't know where I would be today.

When you keep up with children in love, that love makes all the difference. Love reaches out and gets that child when nothing else can help. Love can lift a child out of what he or she is about to do wrong. Love lifted me out again and again. When

I was about to do some misdeed, the thought of my mother's love would lift me out of it.

WITHOUT UNDERSTANDING

Many people are without understanding in America and abroad. In one country where we were holding a crusade, the Lord told me the preachers and their members were like little children without understanding. They had been taught that witchcraft and the Bible went together, and they hadn't studied their Bibles. I don't know how old some of those preachers were when they got their first Bible, but they probably didn't have godly parents to teach them the Word. Although without understanding, they didn't have reprobate minds. Darkness was there, but they were delivered because they met truth and accepted it.

And ye shall know the truth, and the truth shall make you free (John 8:32). The reason some people can never get free is that they don't want truth. They won't accept the truth about their mouth; they won't accept the truth about what they say on the job, off the job or wherever. God doesn't excuse you for gossiping; yet some will do it, forever hurting people.

Untold hours have been wasted because of church people running off at the mouth and disobeying God. There is no heaven for people with a vain religion.

Preacher, I don't do all those things.

No, but are you doing some of them? Not one speck of sin can get through the gates of Glory; the Lord emphatically lets you know that.

When you're without understanding you don't know what the will of God is; you don't realize what you're doing wrong because you won't accept the truth. Do you think you're exempt from the truth?

Parents, are you at fault for not disciplining your children? Do you correct them when you hear them on the telephone criticizing others?

If we had difficulty or trouble in our family, it was kept in the family and before God. That was good training for my mind as a youngster; we didn't talk family problems, not even to Grandma, Grandpa, aunts or uncles. We saw them a lot, but we didn't tell them anything but the good; that's the way God wants it.

You who are raising children now, listen to what they are saying as much as possible. They shouldn't be carrying on a conversation they don't want you to tune in to.

But, Preacher, that's invading their privacy.

Who are you? Are you the parent, or does your child have authority over you? Why did God make moms and dads in the first place, pray tell me? And where in the Bible does it say that children are supposed to be in the driver's seat? Many advertisers cater to the young because, unfortunately, the children rule the roost in so many homes.

Some of you let your children complain, but they'll then become habitual complainers when they're grown. Never let your children complain about their food, for example. I don't know how many times I heard Mama say—and a lot of times it was to me—*When you get hungry enough, Honey, you'll eat it.* She was usually right, too. But I wanted her to feel sorry for me and make something different.

I was aggressive and would have liked to have had my way many times, but I got knocked down—Boom! However, I'd rise back up a little later. Mama used a lot of patience raising me; she had to have a lot. Tribulation worketh patience, and Mama knew when she'd pray for patience, that tribulation was coming. There is a price to pay for patience.

COVENANT BREAKERS

When my parents were out in public and said, *You'll be punished when you get home,* I could feel it then. I hated to hear that. I would suffer and sweat over and over, could almost feel my skin going up and down on my back trying to get out of the way. It was chilling to know that I would get a whipping when I got home. Why didn't they just forget it?—Because they had good understanding from the Lord and they weren't covenant breakers.

Some of you are covenant breakers. You'll tell your children you're going to take a privilege away from them but you don't do it; they know you're not going to do it.

I remember years ago when I was holding a church revival and staying at the parsonage. A neighbor, who lived across the street, saw that her little girl was doing something wrong.

"You get in here!" the mother screamed. "I'm going to pull out every hair on your head!"

The woman could be heard a whole block away. The little girl responded as though the cat had meowed or the poodle had barked one time; she didn't hurry home. I got to thinking about that little girl being bald. The more I thought about it, the funnier it got. When that little girl got to her mother, I doubt she laid a hand on her to pull out even one hair.

I watch things. I like to see how your children respond when you speak to them. When you talk to your children, what happens? How many times do you say you'll do something, but then don't do it?

WITHOUT NATURAL AFFECTION

In so many ways today people are without natural affection. Some people fail to take care of their children. Without natural affection they go off and leave them. They love their pets better than they love their own children. You can ask them where the poodle is and they know, but do they know where their little boy is? *No, where is he? I haven't seen him in the last hour or two. He's every bit of four or five, but he's all right.* Letting children grow up with such little supervision demonstrates a lack of natural affection. That which you love you look after. If you love your husband or wife and your children, you're going to look out for them. If you love God, you're going to look out for Him first and foremost.

On the farm my dad always said we needed a slow rain. If the rain came as a cloudburst, what we called a gully-washer, much of it would run off; but a slow rain would soak into the earth. Are you soaking this in? You need to soak in the truth so you can bless others as well as yourself. Know Jesus, the truth, and be free.

UNMERCIFUL

Many are unmerciful. They can leave their children and not see them for two or three years. Or maybe the devil gets into one mate, and that one takes the children away, bringing great sorrow to the parent who is left behind. The one who does the injustice is unmerciful; the Lord said it would be like that.

When you're unmerciful, you're without love; the Bible tells us that we're nothing without love. **And though I have the gift of prophecy, and understand all mysteries, and all knowledge; and though I have all faith, so that I could remove mountains, and have not charity** [love], **I am nothing** (I Corinthians 13:2).

The Lord let me know a long time ago that in this final hour there would be strict discipline by the Holy Spirit, stricter than you realize. The Lord is bringing these things to you, introducing you to the spirit of man; and, in introducing you to the spirit of man, the devil is uncovered. He has robbed man of the holy human spirit that was given to Adam when he was created in Eden. Guard that holy human spirit you received when you became a new creature in Christ Jesus.

What a plan was given mankind outside of Eden! No one but God could ever have created such a plan of redemption, and no one but God could have made it work. It took all the love of heaven to do it, all the heart of God. God looked at sin, looked at the penalty—death and eternal damnation—and then He looked down through the telescope of time and saw you and me. He knew we would be without understanding like the spirits Jesus preached to in prison;

and, in His great love, God just couldn't forget us, so He made it possible for us to have eternal life. When God sent Jesus, He sent all understanding, wisdom, love, grace, peace, joy, and the whole will of God in one lovely bundle the size of little baby Jesus.

CHAPTER 8

The Deceitfulness Of Sin

God is angry with this old sinful world. Many souls today have gone too far, and God no longer speaks to them or moves for them. They're on their own; they've been turned entirely over to the devil. The Lord will never knock on their heart's door again, never speak to them for all time or eternity. Insulting the blessed Holy Spirit over and over, they have seared their conscience with sin and are without feeling. There's no need for us to worry about them; to worry about any soul that God is finished with is pointless.

In First Timothy, Paul continues writing about the deceitfulness of sin. The latter times refer to these last days we live in, the worst times since Noah's day and the days of Sodom and Gomorrah. **Now the Spirit speaketh expressly** [emphatically, definitely]**, that in the latter times some shall depart from the faith** [the Gospel of Jesus Christ]**, giving heed to seducing spirits, and doctrines of devils** (I Timothy 4:1).

Always remember that it's a doctrine of the devil that claims you can't live free from sin and that God doesn't expect you to live that way. Sin, I say again and again, cannot get into heaven. Those who say it can are repeating a doctrine of devils.

Speaking lies in hypocrisy; having their conscience seared with a hot iron (I Timothy 4:2). Speaking lies until their conscience is seared, people have no feeling; they think they can say anything and do anything against God. That's the reason we have all the murders today, the reason there's so much violence; people don't care. They become so degraded that every thought is evil before God, and God can't stand them. God has already vomited many out of His mouth forevermore.

Forbidding to marry (I Timothy 4:3). How can we associate with family members who are unmarried but living with a partner as though they were married? If it's in their home, you can't. If they are inviting you to come and recognize them as a married, holy couple, absolutely not! But if you've been invited to someone else's home, such as the grandmother's home, and they show up, too; that's a different story. Or if you are invited to your parents' home and they are there, you can speak to them; but I wouldn't buddy with them. Don't act mean or hateful; just show love. However, I'd want everyone to know that I didn't endorse such a lifestyle, that it isn't right and they'll lose their soul over it.

This world has gotten so filled with evil that it vexes our righteous souls daily just like it vexed Lot. God got to the place He couldn't stand it, either.

Commanding to abstain from meats, which God hath created to be received with thanksgiving of them which believe and know the truth (I Timothy 4:3). Some people teach that you can't eat meats, can't do this, can't do that, things that God said were all right to do. Going against what God is for, they are accepting what God is against. They've lined up on the devil's side one hundred percent, and God has rejected them. **For every creature of God is good, and nothing to be refused, if it be received with thanksgiving: For it is sanctified by the word of God and prayer** (I Timothy 4:4,5).

The Lord tells us in the New Testament what is right and what is wrong, what to do and what not to do. The Old Testament is our schoolmaster to help us understand the difference between Law and grace.

Look at the benefits and freedom for people in the light of Calvary and compare them to the limitations of those who lived before Christ. God wants us to be blood conscious, to know that all who want Christ can be made partakers of the divine blood.

MORE WORKS OF THE FLESH IN PERILOUS TIMES

This know also, that in the last days perilous times shall come (II Timothy 3:1). The last days are the same as the latter days, and we have entered perilous and unusually dangerous times. Feeling so secure, we never dreamed that those two New York Trade Center towers could be destroyed and so many lives snuffed out, never dreamed that kind of terrorism could happen in America.

For men shall be lovers of their own selves, covetous, boasters, proud, blasphemers, disobedient to parents, unthankful, unholy, Without natural affection, trucebreakers, false accusers, incontinent, fierce, despisers of those that are good, Traitors, heady, highminded, lovers of pleasures more than lovers of God; Having a form of godliness, but denying the power thereof: from such turn away.

For of this sort are they which creep into houses, and lead captive silly women laden with sins, led away with divers lusts, Ever learning, and

never able to come to the knowledge of the truth (II Timothy 3:2–7). That describes people today. This is a selfish hour; in many homes there's no happiness, just people loving self, self, self. When parents love self better than they love God, they don't make good parents. Homes are not godly homes like they once were, not homes where children are receiving the kind of Bible teaching that builds good character.

COVETOUS

This is a time of coveting. Husbands and wives are coveting another person's companion; there's never been such a loose, awful time. People delight in taking over that which belongs to somebody else; it's a degraded hour.

BLASPHEMERS

Blasphemers use His name in vain, blaspheming the work of God or the name of God. The only time that they use God's name outside of that is when they are scared about half to death and cry out: *Oh, God, have mercy!*

BY-WORDS

By-words are not edifying. Words like *golly* and *gosh* are substitute names for God; *gee* is a substitute for Jesus; look them up in the dictionary. *Darn* means the same thing as *damn*. My people were very strict about not using these kinds of words. We weren't allowed to say, *I swear.* The first time I heard a Christian say that, I was shocked. But many people use those words and think nothing about it. However, if you'll look them up, you may have second thoughts.

UNTHANKFUL

Keep the unthankful spirit out of you or it will be in your children. Teach your children to be thankful. If you are unthankful, grumble about this or that instead of blessing God, then your children are not going to be thankful either.

Don't grumble and complain in front of anyone, especially your children. In fact, you should not complain at all. You never hear your heavenly Father complaining.

So many people are not at all thankful to God in this last hour; and, if you're not careful, it will rub off on you. I say again, be careful whom you associate with, even if they are blood kin.

Before I was saved, my older brother and I would run around together, go to places of the world. He had come back from military service, and I was at an age to go out on the town; we thought we were having some great times. But when God saved me, I never went anywhere else with him—unless he was in the same car when we were going to church. He would have been shocked had I gone anywhere else with him; he understood.

We shared a room with one bed; for years half that bed had been mine and the other half his. We knew which half belonged to whom, and we were supposed to stay on our own side. When I was saved I loved to pray aloud; I would get down by my side of the bed and be praying away while he was in bed. I wasn't doing it for a show; it was my half of the bed. He was used to prayer in our home and wouldn't have expected less out of me. And thank God, one day he did get saved. Isn't that wonderful!

UNHOLY

The Lord said this would be an hour of unholiness. There has been unholiness down through these thousands of years but not like today and not like in Noah's day when the Lord rejected everyone but eight souls. What people did in Noah's day—the hideous, lustful sins people committed—they are doing today.

TRUCE BREAKERS

The Lord gave Paul the revelation that truce breaking also would be in the last days. A person's word is no longer dependable, even the word of some Christians. Do you make promises and not keep them? Are you a promise keeper or a promise breaker? If you don't keep your promises, God cannot keep the good promises He has made to you because you don't qualify for them.

When you make a promise, keep it. Your word should be better than any contract you could ever sign. Many contracts can be broken; people go into bankruptcy and get out of contracts, but for the Holy Spirit to live and dwell in you, your word should be good just like God's is good. Remember, all liars are going to be cast into the lake of fire.

When you don't keep your promise, you're dishonest. God will judge, and you had better take heed.

FALSE ACCUSERS

Those who accuse God's people falsely are liars. The devil can laugh, run, even close his eyes, but he can't live holy. Living holy is what counts. It doesn't matter what people say about you; they said all kinds of awful things about Jesus. He's been back in heaven two thousand years and people still talk against Him, still lie about Him. Pay no attention to false accusers.

Be careful not to falsely accuse someone in your own home. Jealousy is a terrible demon; you can accuse your mate of infidelity when he or she is not guilty at all. The devil will make you think your mate is having an affair when your mate hasn't even seriously looked at anyone else; the devil is trying to stir up dissension to separate you.

Young people, wait for the mind of God to direct you to the right mate, and then you can trust that mate. For twenty-seven years I never had one thought of not being able to trust Angel. I had all confidence that she was pure when I married her, that she would be pure all the days of her life, and that she was. We married in the divine will of God.

People make their own decisions and then blame God when things don't work out. The Bible teaches that sin is to blame for all sorrows, heartaches, sufferings, sicknesses and diseases. God help us in this hour!

Christian, you're either going to take the mind of Jesus in this last hour or you're going to be in grave, grave danger. The devil will put depraved thoughts in you if he is able. The wrong things on the Internet can give you a depraved mind; you don't even have to go out of your house to get it.

A VICIOUS MIND

This is the reprobate mind that I warned against earlier, a mind rejected by God, excluded from salvation and lost in sin. A vicious person is already condemned; God doesn't want them.

It's hard for God to give up on a soul, very hard; I try to never give up on a soul unless God has given up. I must always be willing to give up on any soul that God gives up on.

God has already seen many go to damnation. A news story one time told how about a hundred were killed in a nightclub fire; and the devil probably got them all. If you desire to be in a place like that, you're in the flesh; and you had better sincerely fast and pray until that desire leaves you, until it all goes. Think about the load of souls the devil was getting at one time; terrible screaming went up in that burning building as people were entering a place called hell where Jesus said the fire is never quenched.

INCONTINENT

According to Webster, incontinent means without self-restraint, especially in regard to sexual activities. AIDS is raging throughout the world, affecting the guilty and innocent alike because there's been no restraint on sexual activity. Most young people today haven't been taught chastity; they haven't accepted it. The spirit of the devil has blinded their eyes. Without the grace of God in their spirits, they want to be like the world.

Remember, Israel wanted to be like other nations. They came to Samuel with a request: **Now make us a king to judge us like all the nations. But the thing displeased Samuel, when they said, Give us a king to judge us. And Samuel prayed unto the LORD. And the LORD said unto Samuel, Hearken unto the voice of the people in all that they say unto thee: for they have not rejected thee, but they have rejected me, that I should not reign over them. According to all the works which they have done since the day that I brought them up out of Egypt even unto this day, wherewith they have forsaken me, and served other gods, so do they also unto thee. Now therefore hearken unto their voice: howbeit yet protest solemnly unto them, and shew them the manner of the king that shall reign over them** (I Samuel 8:5–9).

God didn't want Israel to have a king; just about every king they'd had gave them trouble. Look at Ahab; he had brought Baal worship in through his wife, Jezebel. Israel's kings were their great downfall. The people wanted their own way; they had no self-restraint. Samuel cried and cried to God, and the Lord told him, *It's not you, Samuel; they're rejecting me.* Israel got their wish, but it brought much turmoil and suffering.

The Lord has warned you that the time will come you'll regret very much the evil that you did, the times you lacked self-restraint. The Bible says, **Remember now thy Creator in the days of thy youth, while the evil days come not, nor the years draw nigh, when thou shalt say, I have no pleasure in them** (Ecclesiastes 12:1).

It's a loose time; where are your morals? How is your character? What kind of fiber are you made of? Have you really been born new? God has furnished everything to make you just as holy as the first man and woman before the fall. You've been offered the same kind of mind, the mind of Christ, and been offered the same divine blood. When the divine blood that flowed in the veins of Adam and Eve flows in your soul, you'll have the same nature as they had, a divine nature.

Man, created through divinity, was always to have had a divine nature. That divine nature is available to us today; there is no excuse for anyone under this Grace Dispensation to reject it. Grace is freely shared, freely given, freely furnished by heaven through a loving God who never sleeps, never even nods, whose only begotten Son was scarred for us.

After two thousand years, Jesus still ministers

with the Father, stands at His right hand making intercession; the nail prints are in His hands and feet, the scar in His side from whence the Church was born. Think how many times in twenty-four hours the Father has to look at those scars, the only ugly thing in heaven. Jesus was crucified so we could be made beautiful in the eyes of God. When we stand in heaven there will be no scars on us. Never forget Jesus on this journey. We owe everything to the Lord, our very life, all of it.

How set apart are you? Is your obligation more to God or to your kinfolk? Christ didn't shoulder any obligations to His kin that would distract Him from His purpose of redemption for whosoever would come to Him. He was told one time: **Behold, thy mother and thy brethren stand without, desiring to speak with thee. But he answered and said unto him that told him, Who is my mother? and who are my brethren? And he stretched forth his hand toward his disciples, and said, Behold my mother and my brethren! For whosoever shall do the will of my Father which is in heaven, the same is my brother, and sister, and mother** (Matthew 12:47–50). You can't let father, mother, brother, sister or anyone else stand between you and God.

FIERCE

Haven't people always been fierce? What does it mean to be fierce? A fierce nature is violent, cruel, that old sinful Adamic nature; nothing but the divine blood of Jesus can take it out of you. To be fierce is to have a savage, wildly uncontrollable nature. Some people say they just can't help but "blow up". Well, they have to have that fierceness in them to blow up—and that's dangerous. Why would they want to carry anything so dangerous? Why would they flirt with eternal death? Why would they keep giving in to the devil? He is convincing them that they're going to be all right, but they aren't going to be all right; the devil will get them, and he knows it.

DESPISERS OF THOSE WHO ARE GOOD

This is a time of hatred; some of your own blood kin don't like you, much less love you. They'd prefer you weren't invited to their gatherings at Christmas, Thanksgiving, weddings or other special days; or, at best, they wish you wouldn't show up. They simply despise the goodness in you. You're a wet blanket to them because you're set apart from all sin, sanctified and holy unto the Lord.

There's no need to sit around and cry because members of your family mistreat you. Christ was **despised and rejected of men; a man of sorrows,**

and acquainted with grief (Isaiah 53:3), but He didn't let it stop Him. You have to decide that if people don't like you because of the way you serve your God, because of the Gospel that you've accepted in your heart, that's fine; be happy with Jesus. You don't enjoy them and they don't enjoy you; why be a burden to each other?

Some of you obligate yourself to a pit of misery. Every time you go back to a resentful family you're just asking for misery—and they think you enjoy it; that's the reason they give you so much of it. Learn to stand on your own feet with the Lord. Jesus said, **If the Son therefore shall make you free, ye shall be free indeed** (John 8:36). Have you let Jesus set you completely free? Are you miserable, depressed and oppressed much of the time? You should shout, *Hallelujah! I'm free!*

The cry is, *Wake up!* Jesus is coming for those who are watching for Him. Are you going to let the Rapture take place and be left here? Why hold on to anyone who would keep you out of the Rapture?

TRAITORS

Are you around people who would betray you, sell you downstream in a hurry and not even try to protect your life? Some of them would be glad to see you dead, but do you face these things? Live in the tenth chapter of Matthew. The men who made great apostles came out the Jesus way, and it wasn't because they were all that good in the beginning. It took time for the Lord to make a Simon, and He was not able to do it before the Resurrection. Jesus did His best work on Simon Peter after the Resurrection.

Jesus is your Lord, Savior, Master, Director, coming King, strength, power, and love. He qualified in everything; He met the test. Jesus met the devil head-on for you and me and conquered. He proved to us that the devil is just a weakling, a no-good; the devil could not stand up against Him.

We all have our Judases; we've all been betrayed in life. Jesus was betrayed by His own disciple. Traitors are cunning in this last hour. They'll take every dime they can get out of you. Maybe they'll promise to pay you back, but they're not intending to do it. They'll have you sign for them to buy something but then won't reimburse you; they're traitors.

We used to think it was awful if we heard about a traitor to our country, but now it's a daily thing. People in high places in the government are selling us down the river. God help us to get ourselves under the control of the Holy Spirit.

HEADY

To be heady is to be rash, reckless, willful, impetuous. Check to see if you have any of that spirit. The devil will seek to contaminate you just a little bit if he can, as spelled out in my book *Leeching of the Mind*. The devil is cunning; and remember, if you're around his stench, you'll begin to smell bad.

Are you rash, reckless, willful? Have you decided, *I'll do what I want to do and it's none of your business! I'm free; I'm an adult now, and I'll do as I please!* We can't be that way in the hand of the Lord, not at all.

HIGH-MINDED

Haughty, having pride in self, people can be so proud that they won't bow and humble themselves before the Almighty. That's one hundred percent devil pride. God's pride is upright and edifying, beautiful and helpful. God's pride helps us to take more interest in His work, in doing it just right.

I've taken over the work of other people—and Angel did, too—because they wouldn't do it with a whole heart; their hearts weren't really in it. If your heart isn't in doing something for God, you're not going to do it right, and what a shame. Maybe that doesn't affect you, but it affects me. I'm possessed by His love.

But evil men and seducers shall wax worse and worse, deceiving, and being deceived (II Timothy 3:13). Evil seducers are deceiving people. Some preachers have deceived people until their own hearts are so deceived that they declare they are all right. The devil, of course, agrees with them. He has them thoroughly convinced that nothing they do will send them to hell, and they wax worse and worse, seducing and being seduced. What a terrible hour!

Second Timothy is Paul's final letter; in it he pours out his heart to Timothy. **And they shall turn away their ears from the truth, and shall be turned unto fables** (II Timothy 4:4). Many churches today are a part of the world church because they have turned their ears away from the truth.

Are you listening to the truth? Have you really examined yourself? Have you checked your life to see if you are contaminated with any of these sins or influenced by them? Are you being influenced, maybe even by your own kin, to think that God won't send people to hell if they do some of these things? Do you allow for sin in any small measure, not to speak of a big measure? When preachers make allowances for sin, teaching that people can't live free from sin, they cause the damnation of many souls. That doctrine has sent millions and millions of souls to hell these past two thousand years, and it is still raging in these latter times.

A man from a large church not many miles from here said, "Oh, I couldn't go to a church like Grace Cathedral; you have to live too holy." His church teaches that you can't live free from sin; it doesn't preach the pure Gospel. I cannot repeat too often: **The soul that sinneth, it shall die** (Ezekiel 18:20).

Be not deceived; God is not mocked: for whatsoever a man [and that means woman, too] **soweth, that shall he** [or she] **also reap. For he that soweth to his flesh shall of the flesh reap corruption; but he that soweth to the Spirit shall of the Spirit reap life everlasting** (Galatians 6:7,8). If you sow to the flesh, the Bible says you'll reap corruption. If you sow to death, you reap death; and if you sow to life you reap life. For a bountiful crop you had better sow the right seed.

This is one of the last things Paul said to Timothy in the final chapter of Second Timothy: **For Demas hath forsaken me, having loved this present world** (II Timothy 4:10). Demas had been traveling with Paul, and Paul trusted and loved him dearly. Demas had been special. The Bible lets us know that Paul had sent Demas and Luke forth to work together. Imagine how Luke felt when he heard Demas had forsaken Paul!

At one time Demas was dedicated to the Lord and separated from the world, but he got tired of the persecutions, tired of giving of himself; and he became contaminated.

JESUS MUST BECOME REAL

Do you study the Scriptures? Do you hear the voice of the Lord from heaven telling you these things? The Bible is God's voice from heaven to you, but how many of God's people really accept it that way? If the Lord would appear in a bodily form, it wouldn't be hard for them to listen; but they don't let the Bible become that real. When I pick up the Bible I pick up Jesus in living reality. Jesus is this Gospel; He is in this Will of the New Covenant. It's all Jesus. The whole life of Jesus, the whole love that He had in heaven through His heavenly Father is given to us in this Gospel. All the greatness of divine blood is in everything we have today through Jesus.

Paul said, **I can do all things through Christ which strengtheneth me** (Philippians 4:13). Christ is the one who gives the strength. Paul had been through much at that time, but he always kept this in his heart: *I can do all things through Jesus!* Do you often say that you can't do this or you can't do that? You can do it through Jesus.

Preacher, I can't forgive that person.

Through Jesus you can forgive. Don't try to do it in your own strength; it's not your will but His that worketh within you to automatically give you the strength of heaven to do the will of the Lord. The words of Paul are wonderful instructions to remember.

Ask, Jesus said. **All things, whatsoever ye shall ask in prayer, believing, ye shall receive** (Matthew 21:22). If you ask for the will of God, you'll get the will of God. However, many of you don't recognize God's will when it doesn't match your own. Do you really prefer your own will above God's will? Some people talk to me, and I know they want their own will; they just think they want the will of God. God has to wait until they truly want His will.

The love bridle is the will of God. You have one tongue to bridle, but how much do you want it bridled? The tongue is destructive if it's not bridled. You carry either an instrument of destruction or an instrument of edification in your mouth. That of edification includes peace, love, help, and the message for the lost. Unless you have the love bridle, you don't have the real message for the lost, you just have words. The power in your voice to deliver God's message is not there. Why? You're not obedient to God; you talk, tell things about people, and I hear about it. You'd be surprised what I have to listen to that people have told. It's not as bad as it used to be, but there are a few who still talk about others no matter how much God is against it.

Oh, Preacher, I only tell the truth.

But are you telling the truth in love? Does it bless and edify? If not, there's something inside you unlike Jesus, and it comes out.

There should be no confusion, no misgivings or conflict in the body of Christ. Children of God must be healthy in the Lord, clear-eyed with the knowledge and love of Jesus Christ; they must be living, walking epistles in these latter days.

The latter times, I say again, are here, and what filth these days contain! Why plan to mix and mingle with that filth? The night isn't for Christians to go into but for people to come out of. If people want Christian fellowship, they must live holy. Not compromising to be like the world, show all love and grace; give people an opportunity to find Jesus. With love, deliver the milk and honey of salvation that Isaiah the prophet wrote about: **Ho, every one that thirsteth, come ye to the waters, and he that hath no money; come ye, buy, and eat; yea, come, buy wine and milk without money and without price. Wherefore do ye spend money for that which is not bread? and your labour for that which sat-**

isfieth not? hearken diligently unto me, and eat ye that which is good, and let your soul delight itself in fatness (Isaiah 55:1,2). Behold the milk and honey, and come; buy it without price. In other words, salvation from the Rock, Christ Jesus, is free. What a Jesus! What a Christ!

Do you caress and hold onto bad thoughts, or do you want to get rid of them as fast as you can? Do you ask the Holy Spirit for help to flush bad thoughts out of your mind? Are you careful with your mind and with your ears? Jesus said, **He that hath an ear, let him hear what the Spirit saith unto the churches** (Revelation 2:7).

The Spirit is saying much to you today, and He's separating sin to the left. Don't live on the left side or you'll regret it for all eternity. Live on the right side away from the crowd. **Enter ye in at the strait gate: for wide is the gate, and broad is the way, that leadeth to destruction, and many there be which go in thereat** (Matthew 7:13). The broad way is the easy way, the flesh way.

As Paul was writing his last letter to Timothy, the swordsman was getting ready. Timothy, beloved of Paul, stood by him, never betrayed him or let him down. Paul loved him very much and looked forward to seeing him in Glory where he knew a crown would be waiting. Paul told Timothy, *My dear son in the Lord, keep what you have, hold fast to that which is good,* **For I am now ready to be offered, and the time of my departure is at hand. I have fought a good fight, I have finished my course, I have kept the faith: Henceforth there is laid up for me a crown of righteousness, which the Lord, the righteous judge, shall give me at that day: and not to me only, but unto all them also that love his appearing** (II Timothy 4:6–8).

What Paul said to Timothy, let the Lord say to you: *Child, you've kept the faith, you've fought a good fight, and I have a crown of righteousness waiting for you in Glory, for I know you love my appearing.*

Oh Christian, be a good soldier! Don't become entangled again with the world. **Stand fast therefore in the liberty wherewith Christ hath made us free, and be not entangled again with the yoke of bondage** (Galatians 5:1). Examine yourself daily—your attitudes, your motives, and your thoughts—to know whether or not Christ is really in you, or if you operate through the works of the flesh. The greatest gift Jesus could ever give you is freedom from sin. Have you accepted that loving gift?

You can live free from sin. Jesus came down from heaven and showed you how to do it. Walk in His holy steps and sin no more.

CHAPTER 9

Let Romans Put It All Together

And now we go to the book of Romans. **Paul, a servant of Jesus Christ, called to be an apostle, separated unto the gospel of God** (Romans 1:1). When you're separated unto the Gospel, you're separated from the world, separated from all sin. And you're not separated unto the Gospel until you are separated from all sin.

The Gospel is the blood Gospel; sin can't go through the blood without being destroyed. When you took your life to the Gospel, it destroyed every seed of sin. The Bible tells us that **whosoever is born of God doth not commit sin; for his seed remaineth in him: and he cannot sin, because he is born of God** (I John 3:9). That means you cannot sin as long as you keep the seed of God in you. You have to be able to separate the two seeds, the seed of evil from the seed of righteousness. Jesus brought only the seed of righteousness, and it has destroyed every seed of sin in every life born new and made holy.

And declared to be the Son of God with power, according to the spirit of holiness, by the resurrection from the dead (Romans 1:4). Jesus was declared to be the Son of God with power over all sin. You don't have power over all sin if you have the seed of sin. That seed of sin has to be destroyed according to the spirit of holiness. When we're born new, we're born in righteousness and true holiness.

RESURRECTED INTO NEW LIFE

All of us were born into death; but, because Jesus came and was resurrected through the power of His blood, we were resurrected into His life. He came to bring a new and living way. **By a new and living way, which he hath consecrated for us, through the veil, that is to say, his flesh** (Hebrews 10:20).

By whom we have received grace and apostleship, for obedience to the faith among all nations, for his name (Romans 1:5). Now we have received grace. When you obey God—through the obedient spirit that takes you over when you're born new—you bow to the will of God. As long as you keep that seed of righteousness working within, you will do His will because you want to do His will. The old, sinful you has been crucified and is dead. Although you died, you came into real life through Christ Jesus, the remedy for sin and sickness.

CALLED TO BE FREE FROM SIN

Among whom are ye also the called of Jesus Christ (Romans 1:6). Paul is telling some of the Romans who were free from all sin that they were the called of Jesus Christ. When the Lord calls you, He doesn't call you to sin; He calls you out of sin. He calls you from even the appearance of sin. **Abstain from all appearance of evil** (I Thessalonians 5:22). My associate pastors preach the truth. To have it and live it is the only true way. That's the reason we talk to you about your children, the way they act. They need to be delivered from that seed of sin; if they're not, they'll go to hell. You had better do your best to get the seed of sin conquered in them as they are growing up. My mother and dad did their best to keep the seed of sin from being manifested when we as children were yet sinners.

To all that be in Rome, beloved of God, called to be saints (Romans 1:7). You can't be beloved of God if you have the seed of sin; it won't work. God said, **This is my beloved Son, in whom I am well pleased** (Matthew 3:17). Jesus came to make sons and daughters, but with one seed of sin in you, you're not a beloved child. You can't be a son or daughter of God without being beloved by God; He loves all His children.

We're called to be saints, called to be holy. The Bible tells us, **Be ye holy; for I am holy** (I Peter 1:16).

Grace to you and peace from God our Father, and the Lord Jesus Christ (Romans 1:7). We have grace; it's grace to grace for us. We live in grace, we walk that way, we talk that way, and we work that way. We have the peace of heaven on the inside. As the storms rage, we let the Holy Spirit manifest that peace through us; it's in our souls. Peace comes through the divine blood in our souls. The Holy Spirit flushes out the storm when it starts coming into our minds. He also flushes out the fear. **Let not your heart be troubled, neither let it be afraid** (John 14:27).

For I am not ashamed of the gospel of Christ: for it is the power of God unto salvation to every one that believeth; to the Jew first, and also to the Greek [or the Gentiles] (Romans 1:16). When people are ashamed of the Gospel, Jesus is ashamed of them. If you have one sin in your life, you're ashamed of the Gospel or you would embrace the Gospel and love it as God loves it, as Jesus and the Holy Spirit love it.

Now the Gospel is the power of God, and we're not ashamed of it. We are not ashamed to tell people we are born again in Jesus; we're not ashamed of any of the teachings of Jesus Christ. People in the world church are ashamed of the real Jesus, and so they follow a Jesus of their imagination.

FROM FAITH TO FAITH

First, I thank my God through Jesus Christ for you all, that your faith is spoken of throughout the whole world (Romans 1:8). The people Paul was writing to had the Jesus faith; anything that's not His faith is dead faith. Read it in the second chapter of James for yourself; it's just plain dead faith. **Even so faith, if it hath not works, is dead, being alone. For as the body without the spirit is dead, so faith without works is dead also** (James 2:17,26).

For therein is the righteousness of God revealed from [divine] **faith to** [divine] **faith: as it is written, The just shall live by faith** (Romans 1:17). The righteousness of God cannot be revealed through a human being who has one seed of sin. When you have one seed of sin in you, that seed generates disobedience. You are not living by the faith of God; you're living in your own feelings, following your own heart on the path to hell. That's what people were doing before Jesus came.

You must live by faith. I say again, faith is a gift from God; salvation is a gift from God; love is a gift from God. God will not excuse you for having a seed of sin, not one seed.

For the wrath of God is revealed from heaven against all ungodliness and unrighteousness of men, who hold the truth in unrighteousness (Romans 1:18). You have the wrath of God hovering over your head if you have one seed of sin in you, and His hand of wrath is terrible. In the Old Testament, study the times God used that left hand, that hand of His wrath.

In the book of Acts, we find that, after Pentecost, the Lord had His right hand raised for the followers of Christ; and they went forth conquering. But those who had one sin in them were disobedient to the Gospel, they held His truth in unrighteousness, and their acts were unrighteous.

Paul touched on living free from sin in other epistles that he wrote through the Holy Ghost, but no other writer brought forth sin like he did in Romans.

GOD HATES SIN

For the wrath of God is revealed from heaven against all ungodliness and unrighteousness of men, who hold the truth in unrighteousness (Romans 1:18). Paul, addressing the Christians in Rome, wasn't saying this for just their benefit; he wanted all to hear. Paul probably thought God would surely see to it that the non-Christians would read some of this, too.

Because that which may be known of God is manifest in them; for God hath shewed it unto them. For the invisible things of him from the creation of the world are clearly seen, being understood by the things that are made, even his eternal power and Godhead; so that they are without excuse (Romans 1:19,20). When you see the stars, the moon, the sun, the sky, the clouds, the rain, the snow, the green grass, the birds, and all that God has made, there's no excuse for saying God doesn't exist. A living God has to be behind all of this; He has to give the life that makes the flowers to grow and the birds to fly. God wrote songs for the birds and gave them a voice to sing. He created all the fish in the sea; He is the great Creator. The devil created nothing; he is death, death, death! The devil can't bring up the sun, and he can't put it down. The devil is limited in what he can do; there's no life about him, and he can't heal.

Some knew there was a God; however, they didn't like Him. **Because that, when they knew God, they glorified him not as God, neither were thankful** [speaking of backsliders; they came into the knowledge of God but were not thankful]**; but became vain in their imaginations, and their foolish heart was darkened** (Romans 1:21). *Darkened* means shut out from God. These people Paul was writing about had turned out the lights without any intention of ever turning them back on. They didn't want God, and that's the way people are today. Of the over six billion on planet Earth, it's hard to tell how many billions don't want the true and living God.

They became vain in their imaginations, plotting what they could get by with. The Bible says to cast down imaginations or you will be in big trouble. **Casting down imaginations, and every high thing that exalteth itself against the knowledge of God, and bringing into captivity every thought to the obedience of Christ** (II Corinthians 10:5).

I wish all the young people could read this book on being free from sin because it's coming from God. The darkness has taken over some, and they don't have the light. How pathetic! But I can't spend all my time on them; Jesus is coming, and we've got to get the Gospel to the whole world.

PUSHED OUT OF THE WAY

Professing themselves to be wise, they became fools (Romans 1:22). A fool in the eyes of God is someone without Him. **The fool hath said in his heart, There is no God** (Psalm 14:1). Remember what Job told his wife: **Then said his wife unto him, Dost thou still retain thine integrity? curse God, and die. But he said unto her, Thou speakest as one of the foolish women speaketh** (Job 2:9,10).

Some people profess themselves to be wise, and they think they're getting by. Some are out in the dark now; they don't go to church anymore. If they're not going to live for God and choose to be degraded, we've got to go on.

It's dangerous to be in this congregation [addressing Grace Cathedral congregation] now and not serve God, to deceive yourself and others. God is subject to kill in this hour because He has a body raised up just like He did in the Early Church; it took Him years to bring this body of people together. God told me when I first started the work to not look at the people; He was going to take care of that. He would separate; He would push out and bring in, and He's done just that.

God set this church in order, I didn't. I wait upon Him. At times some people think I don't know what's going on around here because I don't do anything about it, but I'm waiting on God.

This is one dangerous hour; you're either in or you're out with God. If your children are not really in with God, they could be destroyed at any time. Some of them live loose, very loose; they think it's the "in" thing. It is the in thing, but it's of the devil.

And changed the glory of the uncorruptible God into an image made like to corruptible man, and to birds, and fourfooted beasts, and creeping things (Romans 1:23). When the backsliders turned away from the perfect and incorruptible God, they turned to corruption and made their own gods! Think of the useless materials people have used to make gods. God wants you to know He's incorruptible.

Being filled with all unrighteousness, fornication, wickedness, covetousness, maliciousness; full of envy, murder, debate, deceit, malignity; whisperers (Romans 1:29). I've warned people about whispering and gossip. Why would you whisper, pass out deceit and garbage? Whisperers will not go with Jesus when He comes; if they die as whisperers, they won't be in God's heaven but in hell.

THE RESPONSIBILITY OF CHILDREN

Backbiters, haters of God, despiteful, proud, boasters, inventors of evil things, disobedient to parents (Romans 1:30). Disobedient to parents—we have that evil now. Some of you don't control your children from the day they're born. Before they're even walking they're slapping your face. They get mad; I've seen babies so angry and parents let them get by, looking more to psychology and psychiatry than to the Bible.

My mother and dad didn't care anything about psychiatry or psychology, and they wouldn't have thought about taking us to either one. Where I lived as a child, people used the woodshed and the Bible. That section was known as the Bible Belt, but they've lost it and turned their children over to the devil. It's awful to bring children into the world and let them go to hell. My God!

When you bring children into the world, you're responsible for them before God. You've brought a living soul into the world, and they've been born lost. If they die lost, they'll be in hell and the lake of fire as the eternal ages roll. That ought to wake you up. Children must be taught the real Gospel, freedom from all sin, or they will go to hell for sinning against God.

Some parents seem to take pleasure in the ungodly

Chapter 9: Let Romans Put It All Together

acts of their children. The Lord wants you to know that. I didn't ask Him; He just tells me, and He's giving me these thoughts of His. The main goal of my mother and dad was to direct us to heaven. They didn't cram the Gospel down our throats, but they gave us discipline. They did their best to keep us clean. Are you doing your best? People will bring children into the healing line who are three, four, five years of age, and say they can't do anything with them. I'd be ashamed to tell it. I'd do something with them!

Preacher, you never had any children!

No, but I was raised. My mom and dad had me. Sometimes I wished they had not had me, but they did. I didn't get anywhere by saying I wished I'd never been born. I guess they wished that, too, sometimes.

What a responsibility you parents have! Angel and I didn't want that responsibility, and we decided we would not have children. After Angel died, someone said, "What a pity that you and Angel didn't have children!" My God! Had children? I was going through hell after losing her. If I'd had two or three children pulling on me, screaming about their mother dying, it would have been enough to drive me out of my mind! Angel and I would never have been able to help raise as many children as we did if we had had children of our own, and God had a hand in that.

Some people don't believe in birth control, but God does. The Noah family didn't have a baby born into it for a hundred and twenty years. If that's not birth control, what is? Not a child was born until the filth of a sinful civilization was destroyed from the earth. The Lord knew that if the sons of Noah brought children into the world, they could easily become children of hell and destruction, children who would grow up to despise and reject the ways of God.

Some of you think, "Oh, that little darling; the Lord sent him to me!" Then later you think, "Oh, my God, if He did, the angel dropped him and ran!" If you could put a postage stamp on some of yours and send them back, you would, wouldn't you? You might as well fess up to yourself.

THE SEED OF SIN

Who [God] **will render to every man according to his deeds** (Romans 2:6). That means judgment for the seed of sin, one sin.

To them who by patient continuance in well-doing seek for glory and honour and immortality, eternal life: But unto them that are contentious, and do not obey the truth, but obey unrighteous-

ness, indignation and wrath, Tribulation and anguish, upon every soul of man that doeth evil, of the Jew first, and also of the Gentile; But glory, honour, and peace, to every man that worketh good, to the Jew first, and also to the Gentile** (Romans 2:7–10). There's no good in the seed of sin. The Lord told Adam and Eve that the seed of sin was on the tree of death.

But he is a Jew, which is one inwardly; and circumcision is that of the heart, in the spirit, and not in the letter; whose praise is not of men, but of God (Romans 2:29). The circumcision of the body won't save you. Circumcision of the flesh should be used only for health's sake; it's circumcision of the heart that we need, and that circumcision comes through the blood of Jesus. Every evil seed, no matter how tiny, is destroyed with that circumcision of the heart, completely destroyed.

As it is written, There is none righteous, no, not one (Romans 3:10). Continue to follow this carefully now.

There is none that understandeth, there is none that seeketh after God. They are all gone out of the way [of God], **they are together become unprofitable; there is none that doeth good, no, not one. Their throat is an open sepulchre; with their tongues they have used deceit; the poison of

asps is under their lips [That's the poison tongue of backbiters and gossips]: **Whose mouth is full of cursing and bitterness: Their feet are swift to shed blood: Destruction and misery are in their ways: And the way of peace have they not known: There is no fear of God before their eyes** (Romans 3:11–18). This is describing people without God who have never known what it means to be holy. They came into the world unholy, and most stayed unholy.

Now we know that what things soever the law saith, it saith to them who are under the law: that every mouth may be stopped, and all the world may become guilty before God. Therefore by the deeds of the law there shall no flesh be justified in his sight: for by the law is the knowledge of sin (Romans 3:19,20). When the Law was put into practice it uncovered what God calls sin.

But now the righteousness of God without the law is manifested, being witnessed by the law and the prophets (Romans 3:21). Grace came and fulfilled the Law, but it didn't do away with sin; sin is still sin.

Even the righteousness of God which is by faith of Jesus Christ unto all and upon all them that believe: for there is no difference: For all have sinned, and come short of the glory of God

(Romans 3:22,23). This scripture is misused when people say that the Bible states everyone sins (present tense). No, it says all *have* sinned (past tense). Before we were saved we had all sinned, but we can be born new. Those who are truly born again no longer sin.

JUSTIFIED BY GRACE

Being justified freely by his grace through the redemption that is in Christ Jesus (Romans 3:24). We are justified freely by God's grace, delivered from every seed of sin through the redemption that is in Christ Jesus, the Second Adam. The first Adam was created in perfection but failed; the Second Adam came in perfection and did not fail. He made it possible for all to come into perfection.

Whom God hath set forth to be a propitiation through faith in his blood, to declare his righteousness for the remission of sins that are past, through the forbearance of God; To declare, I say, at this time his righteousness: that he might be just, and the justifier of him which believeth in Jesus (Romans 3:25,26). We're justified only by having the shed blood of Jesus in our souls; we're not justified without divine blood.

Where is boasting then? It is excluded. By what law? of works? Nay: but by the law of faith

(Romans 3:27). Some boast that they're keepers of the Law of Moses, but that isn't enough or Jesus would not have come. Paul separated Law and grace and made it clear that Jesus brought the law of love.

Therefore we conclude that a man is justified by faith without the deeds of the law (Romans 3:28). The Law has nothing to do with justification; the Law is the schoolmaster that brings us up to the Gospel.

Is he the God of the Jews only? is he not also of the Gentiles? Yes, of the Gentiles also: Seeing it is one God, which shall justify the circumcision by faith, and uncircumcision through faith. Do we then make void the law through faith? God forbid: yea, we establish the law (Romans 3:29-31). We establish in our faith that God condemns sin. God once had sinners stoned and put to death, but not today. However, sin is still sin in the eyes of God, and judgment will come.

Jesus is holding back judgment, which is very deceiving to many preachers and laymen. The Lord stands between them and judgment, or else God would have already destroyed many, many people as He did under the Law. People were stoned to death for adultery and whoredom and killed for all kinds of other sins. The Lord even opened the ground at times, and it swallowed up people by the thousands. **And the earth opened her mouth, and swallowed them up, and their houses, and all the men that appertained unto Korah, and all their goods. They, and all that appertained to them, went down alive into the pit, and the earth closed upon them: and they perished from among the congregation** (Numbers 16:32,33).

Because of David's sin, over seventy thousand men were killed. Think about it! **So the LORD sent a pestilence upon Israel from the morning even to the time appointed: and there died of the people from Dan even to Beer-sheba seventy thousand men. And when the angel stretched out his hand upon Jerusalem to destroy it, the LORD repented him of the evil, and said to the angel that destroyed the people, It is enough: stay now thine hand. And the angel of the LORD was by the threshingplace of Arau-nah the Jeb-u-site. And David spake unto the LORD when he saw the angel that smote the people, and said, Lo, I have sinned, and I have done wickedly: but these sheep, what have they done? let thine hand, I pray thee, be against me, and against my father's house** (II Samuel 24:15–17).

Study God in this light; *many people never have, saith the Lord.* They think that God is not doing anything because He doesn't strike anyone dead; they think He's not going to bring any judgment. That's what the devil is telling people, and that's false believing.

Blessed are they whose iniquities are forgiven, and whose sins are covered. Blessed is the man to whom the Lord will not impute sin (Romans 4:7,8). When God covers your sins, they're not in your life anymore; they're gone, cast into the sea of forgetfulness. Now your sins are as far from you as the East is from the West. Blessed is that man whom God will not accuse of one seed of sin.

And being not weak in faith, he [Abraham] **considered not his own body now dead, when he was about an hundred years old** [he couldn't look at that], **neither yet the deadness of Sarah's womb: He staggered not at the promise of God through unbelief; but was strong in faith, giving glory to God** (Romans 4:19,20). Abraham staggered not at the promise of God. There is a great lesson here, a vital one that many people have overlooked. You've got to look at God and His promises. You can't look at your imperfections, your weaknesses, and decide whether or not God will keep His promises. You can't use the failure of people to keep their promises to decide whether or not God will keep His.

God tells us that He is not a man. **God is not a**

man, that he should lie; neither the son of man, that he should repent: hath he said, and shall he not do it? or hath he spoken, and shall he not make it good** (Numbers 23:19)?

WAVERING FAITH IS USELESS

The Bible tells us that if our faith wavers, we are not to think we will receive anything from God. **But let him ask in faith, nothing wavering. For he that wavereth is like a wave of the sea driven with the wind and tossed. For let not that man think that he shall receive any thing of the Lord** (James 1: 6,7). If you don't have perfect faith in God, there's something wrong with you.

And being fully persuaded that, what he had promised, he was able also to perform (Romans 4:21). Abraham was fully persuaded, not by looking at his dead body or Sarah's dead body, but by looking at the promises of God.

You can't look to self but only to Calvary to get forgiveness of your sins; look with godly sorrow. There's no need to pray unless you have godly sorrow. If you're not as sorry for your sins and disobediences as God is, He won't forgive you. Without godly sorrow you would just go forth to do more sin.

Therefore being justified by faith, we have

peace with God through our Lord Jesus Christ (Romans 5:1). When you're justified in the eyes of God, there's no condemnation, the seed of sin is not there or Eve would have been justified at the tree of death. But she accepted the seed of sin even though the Lord had said it would kill her. If you have the seed of sin, just one seed, it kills and will take all the life from you.

By whom also we have access by faith into this grace wherein we stand, and rejoice in hope of the glory of God (Romans 5:2). How do we stand? We stand by faith in this divine grace and divine faith.

TRIBULATION BRINGS PATIENCE

And not only so, but we glory in tribulations also: knowing that tribulation worketh patience [divine patience] (Romans 5:3). In your patience you possess everything heavenly, everything great, everything needed.

And patience [worketh]**, experience; and experience, hope** (Romans 5:4). This is all divinity.

And hope maketh not ashamed; because the love of God is shed abroad in our hearts by the Holy Ghost which is given unto us (Romans 5:5). We come into the reality of divine hope **because the love of God is shed abroad in our hearts by the Holy Ghost**. The Holy Ghost cannot shed abroad the love of God in your heart if the heart is not clean and pure. If your heart has a seed of sin, it's contaminated and the Holy Ghost cannot shed abroad the love of God.

The love of God and one speck of sin, one tiny seed of sin, will not mix. You either have the love of God, or you don't have the love of God. If you don't have the love of God, you don't have salvation.

When you're aware of that seed of sin, you must get rid of it. However, if you're not aware of the seed of sin, yield to the Holy Ghost; He'll let you know that there's no life in sin, just death, death, death; that's the judgment voice of God even before your soul leaves the body. Today, there are more dead people walking around, spiritually speaking, than you'll ever find alive. Are you alive today, or are you dead? You can't be halfway between; you're either alive or dead.

For when we were yet without strength, in due time Christ died for the ungodly. For scarcely for a righteous man will one die: yet peradventure for a good man some would even dare to die (Romans 5:6,7). Jesus died for us, and the Lord says there's no excuse not to love Him and reject sin.

But God commendeth his love toward us, in that, while we were yet sinners, Christ died for us (Romans 5:8). When you have sin in your heart, you're a sinner; at one time we all were sinners. But when you're born again, you are no longer a sinner. Christ died to provide saving grace to all who would accept it. Paul is writing to holy people living free from sin.

The Christians at Rome were living free from sin, and Rome is where many of them were put to death. They never would have died for the sake of Christ with one seed of sin in them. Not one hypocrite or one sinner was willing to die for the sake of Christ. It was the seed of righteousness that gave them God's heart, God's love, God's divine faith, God's divine goodness, God's divine mercy and strength. All this caused them to give their lives. Burned at the stake, fed to the lions, Christians were martyred in all kinds of cruel ways; but many Christians, as long as they had voice, rejoiced and sang the praises of God. My God!

Much more then, being now justified by his blood, we shall be saved from wrath through him (Romans 5:9). Notice now, we're justified by His blood; that's the way to be free of condemnation. One seed of sin brings condemnation. Go to the Garden and you'll find that condemnation and judgment went into action at once. Condemnation in Noah's day drowned thousands and saved just eight souls. Condemnation in Lot's day destroyed

Sodom and Gomorrah.

For if, when we were enemies, we were reconciled to God by the death of his Son, much more, being reconciled, we shall be saved by his life (Romans 5:10). When you have the seed of sin, you're an enemy to God; He doesn't count you as a son or daughter. No, you have to be free from all sin to be a son or daughter of God, to be in the family of God.

THE ATONEMENT

And not only so, but we also joy in God through our Lord Jesus Christ, by whom we have now received the atonement (Romans 5:11). Notice, we have the atonement, a twofold atonement for the whole person, soul and body. If you've received the atonement, you're holy, but you must keep the atonement; it has to abide in you forever. If you don't keep it, you won't make it to heaven.

Wherefore, as by one man sin entered into the world, and death by sin; and so death passed upon all men, for that all have sinned (Romans 5:12). How did sin come into the world of the human race? One man accepted that seed from the devil, from the tree of death, and it brought all of this damnable suffering upon the human race. Think what a day that was! God surely cried—God the Father,

God the Son, God the Holy Ghost and the angels.

Sin had entered the whole human race now, and every child would be conceived in sin and iniquities and would need a Savior. But did they want a Savior? Did they have the right kind of mother and father? Adam and Eve did not make good parents.

Make sure you're a good parent; know the responsibility you have when you bring a child into the world. God brought Adam and Eve into the world, and He gave them His whole heart, all of His love. Later, He gave His Son to make it possible for humanity to escape hell and the lake of fire. What a price when sin is involved! My Lord!

(For until the law sin was in the world: but sin is not imputed when there is no law. Nevertheless death reigned from Adam to Moses, even over them that had not sinned after the similitude of Adam's transgression, who is the figure of him that was to come (Romans 5:13,14). Death reigned even over people who did not sin—Abraham and others.

But not as the offence, so also is the free gift. For if through the offence of one many be dead, much more the grace of God, and the gift by grace, which is by one man, Jesus Christ, hath abounded unto many (Romans 5:15). Through one came the seed of death; and through one came the seed of life. Jesus brought nothing but life; He came with the seed of righteousness, which Adam and Eve were created with but lost.

Think about the great price paid by Jesus Christ. That gift is for everybody, but such a few will use it. By not using it, you use the tree of death. Think of the hordes of people who are in hell today or are on their way. God has had just about all that He can take of it; and, like in Noah's day, it's almost time for destruction. But first the Bride will be taken out. Are you ready for the Bride to go? Are you going to be a member of the bridal company?

DELIVERANCE IS OFFERED TO THE SINNER

And not as it was by one that sinned, so is the gift: for the judgment was by one to condemnation, but the free gift is of many offences unto justification (Romans 5:16). It doesn't matter how many sins you have committed; deliverance and help are offered to you.

For if by one man's offence death reigned by one; much more they which receive abundance of grace and of the gift of righteousness shall reign in life by one, Jesus Christ (Romans 5:17). Through Jesus Christ we will reign in life—not death—as the eternal ages roll. Those who reject Him have no hope; they will reign in death for all eternity . . . death, death, death and no life. Imagine that desolation: no flowers, no trees, no sunshine, no rain, no green grass, no animals, no fish, no water, nothing but desolation.

Therefore as by the offence of one judgment came upon all men to condemnation [because of Adam's sin]**; even so by the righteousness of one the free gift came upon all men unto justification of life** (Romans 5:18). This is a profound verse. Everyone is offered justification. The sign went up: *whosoever will*. **And the Spirit and the bride say, Come. And let him that heareth say, Come. And let him that is athirst come. And whosoever will, let him take the water of life freely** (Revelation 22:17).

The tabernacle was built under the Law, but Israel remained a servant; they stood outside. They couldn't get in to God, couldn't talk to God. God would come down one day a year for them, the Day of Atonement. But since Jesus came, every day is a Day of Atonement, one in which the sinners can come home. What a tremendous Gospel we have to preach, an incredible Gospel!

For as by one man's disobedience many were made sinners, so by the obedience of one shall many be made righteous (Romans 5:19). Many were condemned through Adam's disobedience;

they followed in his path. Are you disobedient to the call of God? Are you deceived? Are you really obedient to Him, or is self in control? Is self on the altar, or is Jesus on the altar? Is the Holy Spirit really guiding you, making intercession to the Father for you, or are you just stumbling along in the night trying to convince yourself that you're all right? Which is it?

Moreover the law entered, that the offence might abound. But where sin abounded, grace did much more abound (Romans 5:20). Sin was abounding, but grace is greater than all the sin on planet Earth.

That as sin hath reigned unto death, even so might grace reign through righteousness unto eternal life by Jesus Christ our Lord (Romans 5:21).

Study the book of Romans. Oh, what a book this is! The Lord can give you those extra thoughts as you study it. No wonder the Lord said for us to examine ourselves to see if we be in the faith. **Examine yourselves, whether ye be in the faith; prove your own selves. Know ye not your own selves, how that Jesus Christ is in you, except ye be reprobates** (II Corinthians 13:5)?

Are you really in the Jesus faith or not? Consider what a price heaven has paid, what sacrificing has been made for your salvation. How much are you willing to sacrifice?

Where are you today? What if God would call your name and ask, "Where art thou?" Could you say, *I'm in your divine will, Lord. I'm in your divine love where you called me to be! I'm in your divine grace, your divine faith, your divine peace. I have on the shoes of your Son, Jesus. I am clothed in the Gospel of righteousness and holiness. I have no fig leaves and nothing to hide from you, dear God; I have no doubt. I know that I'm not naked, so I'm not trying to cover myself. Your Son brought me a robe of righteousness through His shed blood, and my nakedness is covered. I'm not ashamed of the Gospel of your Son, Jesus Christ. I love your Gospel; I love your people; and I love to do your will, Lord.*

You called me to do your will, called me into your righteousness, your holiness. You called my eyes to holiness; you called my ears to righteousness and holiness. You called my tongue, my voice, and I gave all to you, Lord; and now I have all of Him, your Son, Jesus. I have nothing to fear, nothing to worry about; I'm on my way with this Gospel for the whole world, and on my way to Rapture ground.

The Lord is lifting you, children of God. *He's lifting you, the obedient, to make you sit in heavenly places, saith the Lord.* He is moving for you now, lifting you up, up through the blood Gospel, lifting you higher and higher through the blessed, divine faith and love of Him.

CHAPTER 10

Some Final Words To The Romans

Now we continue in Romans, the great book which talks more against sin than any other book throughout the whole Bible. If we didn't have anything else but the letter that the Lord gave Paul for the Romans, living free from sin would be plain, simple, and clear. How sad that some people don't want the truth. Jesus said, **I am the way, the truth, and the life: no man cometh unto the Father, but by me** (John 14:6). He came to show us how to be free through the truth.

Some people can tell you how to do something, but they can't show you. Jesus already was very God when He took on flesh as we have flesh; and, by becoming very man, He could be touched by the feeling of our infirmities. **For we have not an high priest which cannot be touched with the feeling of our infirmities; but was in all points tempted like as we are, yet without sin** (Hebrews 4:15). Jesus has traveled all our paths.

For even hereunto were ye called: because Christ also suffered for us, leaving us an example, that ye should follow his steps (I Peter 2:21). Christ is our example; follow in His steps.

What shall we say then? Shall we continue in sin, that grace may abound (Romans 6:1)? Isn't that a big question to ask yourself? This is great, wonderful reading.

God forbid. How shall we, that are dead to sin, live any longer therein (Romans 6:2)? When Christ comes into your heart, you die to sin and are resurrected through the blood; you're brought to life.

You came into the world conceived in sin and iniquities. The Bible declares that **all have sinned, and come short of the glory of God** (Romans 3:23). But when you die with Christ Jesus, you die to sin. If you're dead to something, you don't live in it anymore.

Know ye not, that so many of us as were baptized into Jesus Christ were baptized into his death (Romans 6:3)? When you accept Jesus Christ, you are baptized unto His death spiritually through the blood. When you are baptized in water, it's a physical baptism in answer of a clear conscience.

THE NEW AND LIVING WAY

Therefore we are buried with him by baptism into death [in the likeness of death]**: that like as Christ was raised up from the dead by the glory of the Father, even so we also should walk in newness of life** (Romans 6:4). Jesus was raised up by the glory of God in the newness of life. He had conquered death—not for Himself but for you and for me—so now we can walk in the newness of life.

Jesus brought the new and living way, the sinless way. Remember, sin and righteousness will not mix; you're either righteous or unrighteous, holy or unholy, sinless or sinful. Which is it?

For if we have been planted together in the likeness of his death, we shall be also in the likeness of his resurrection (Romans 6:5). You'll not come forth in the resurrection of the righteous unless you have been planted in the likeness of His death. It will not be until after the seven years of the Tribulation Period and the thousand years of the Perfect Age that the wicked dead come forth to the Great White Throne Judgment.

Knowing this, that our old man [that old you

that caused you so much trouble] **is crucified with him, that the body of sin might be destroyed, that henceforth we should not serve sin** (Romans 6:6). How much plainer could living sin-free be? From this time of salvation forward, there is to be no more sinning; that's what the Word of God is saying.

For he that is dead [dead in Christ] **is freed from sin** (Romans 6:7). When you die in Christ, you die out to the world and to all sin. If you're dead in Christ, you're alive in righteousness and holiness, free from all sin.

Now if we be dead with Christ, we believe that we shall also live with him (Romans 6:8). There's no need to believe you're going to live with Him if you're not dead to sin, having died with Christ.

Knowing that Christ being raised from the dead dieth no more; death hath no more dominion over him (Romans 6:9). When we're in Christ, not just sin but even death will have no more dominion over us; we will live forever. **Therefore if any man be in Christ, he is a new creature: old things are passed away; behold, all things are become new** (II Corinthians 5:17). And if any man or woman be in Christ, they will live forever. Jesus said, **Because I live, ye shall live also** (John 14:19).

For in that he died, he died unto sin once: but in that he liveth, he liveth unto God (Romans 6:10).

Jesus was the supreme sacrifice to save us from our sin; He is our atonement. The atoning blood is before the throne for us day and night; we can use it to stay free from sin every moment that we have left on planet Earth.

Likewise reckon ye also yourselves to be dead indeed unto sin, but alive unto God through Jesus Christ our Lord (Romans 6:11). Think about this and reason it out: You're to be just like Jesus. Jesus was dead to all sin; He conquered death, hell, and the grave, and is alive unto the Father forevermore.

Let not sin therefore reign in your mortal body, that ye should obey it in the lusts thereof (Romans 6:12). Don't let any sin be in this body of clay. If you have sin in you, you're going to obey that sin; that's biblical.

The Lord warned Adam and Eve to go only to the tree of life, never to the tree of death; but they went to that tree anyway. Jesus had to die to destroy that tree of death along with its influence and power over our lives, so that we could again go to the tree of life. God sent that tree of life down to us in the form of Jesus. We receive our benefits through Him and from Him.

ALIVE FROM THE DEAD

Neither yield ye your members as instruments of unrighteousness unto sin: but yield yourselves unto God, as those that are alive from the dead, and your members as instruments of righteousness unto God (Romans 6:13). Don't give your hands, your eyes, or your ears over to unrighteousness. You who are in pornography, you're sinning with your eyes and with your ears.

You don't sin through temptation or battles of the mind; you sin if you yield to the seed of sin. We were dead in trespasses, the Bible declares, but now we're alive from the dead. **And you hath he quickened, who were dead in trespasses and sins** (Ephesians 2:1). No longer dead, we yield our members to righteousness as one alive.

Our hands are righteousness unto God. We were not the righteousness of God, but the Bible tells us Jesus came to make us that righteousness. We have to keep Jesus in our lives to keep that righteousness. If we fail Him and sin against His love commandments, we'll lose it all.

For sin shall not have dominion over you (Romans 6:14). That means sin will have no power over you. You don't have to worry about sin; you don't have to be afraid you'll sin. You don't have to walk around like you're walking on eggs; you pick up your feet and put them down in all confidence. With full assurance, faith, and power, you can trample devils underfoot. **Behold, I give unto you power** [said Jesus] **to tread on serpents and scorpions, and over all the power of the enemy: and nothing shall by any means hurt you** (Luke 10:19). The holy mantle that the Lord brought belongs to us; use it!

For ye are not under the law, but under grace (Romans 6:14). In grace there's no sin. There was no sin found in Noah or his family; that's the reason they were saved. God will do anything for a person who is without sin; that right arm will go up with all the powers of heaven in it for each and every little lamb that is wholly His.

This plan of salvation is so fabulous that it takes the Spirit's help for you to comprehend it. Don't say you don't understand, say the Lord will give you understanding. In fastings, prayers, and living in the Word, **study to shew thyself approved unto God, a workman that needeth not to be ashamed, rightly dividing the word of truth** (II Timothy 2:15).

LAW AND GRACE

What then? shall we sin, because we are not under the law, but under grace? God forbid (Romans 6:15). Paul wrote to the people in Rome because they were confused about Law and grace.

Paul knew the Law to the letter. Nobody could explain Law and grace like the apostle Paul. In his left hand was the Law of Moses, and in his right hand were the grace and righteousness of Jesus Christ. Circumcision over here to the left is physical, of the body; circumcision over here to the right is spiritual, of the heart. Everything to the right is spiritual—grace, grace, grace.

Know ye not, that to whom ye yield yourselves servants to obey, his servants ye are to whom ye obey; whether of sin unto death, or of obedience unto righteousness (Romans 6:16)? If you can't live free from sin, you belong to the devil. If you're not free from sin today, you are the devil's merchandise; and, if you die with willful sin in your heart, you will go to hell, not heaven. Only the obedient will go to heaven. With a seed of sin in your heart, you're disobedient to God.

In the beginning, man and woman in the Garden were never disobedient to God; they were just as holy as God, Jesus, and the Holy Spirit. The Lord came down to walk and talk with man and woman in the cool of the day. There was no struggle, no despair, no burdens to bear; everything was joy. Eden was heaven; it was planned to be that way, but man destroyed his own heaven. Many people are destroying their own heaven today.

IS STATIC IN YOUR LIFE?

Ye have obeyed from the heart that form of doctrine which was delivered you (Romans 6:17). You have to obey from the heart.

Some people contend that they're obeying God. King Saul did that with Samuel, but it didn't work. **And Samuel came to Saul: and Saul said unto him, Blessed be thou of the LORD: I have performed the commandment of the LORD. And Samuel said, What meaneth then this bleating of the sheep in mine ears, and the lowing of the oxen which I hear** (I Samuel 15:13,14)? What is all the noise of disobedience? When you're not obedient to God, there's noise and static in your life. I can feel and hear that static again and again in people who say they're doing the will of God when they're not.

Do you always tell them, Preacher?

No, not everyone is ready for it. If God can't let you know, why would I try? God uses me to get into people who can be reached, but if they can't be reached, God doesn't use me for them.

Being then made free from sin, ye became the servants of righteousness (Romans 6:18). To me this is plain; it's ignorance on the part of people when they don't want to understand plain English.

Jesus said, **No man can serve two masters: for either he will hate the one, and love the other; or else he will hold to the one, and despise the other. Ye cannot serve God and mam-mon** (Matthew 6:24). You can't hold to both righteousness and unrighteousness, holiness and unholiness.

I speak after the manner of men because of the infirmity of your flesh: for as ye have yielded your members servants to uncleanness and to iniquity unto iniquity; even so now yield your members servants to righteousness unto holiness (Romans 6:19). Don't go from righteousness to disobedience and sin; go from righteousness to holiness, that's all that God will accept. Look at the price that was paid: God gave Jesus, His heart, so that we could be made the righteousness of God. Without Jesus, we would be anything but the righteousness of God.

For when ye were the servants of sin, ye were free from righteousness (Romans 6:20). When you were a sinner, there was no righteousness in you. I say again sin and righteousness will not mix. When you were the servant of sin, you were free from righteousness.

Most people and even most preachers are free from righteousness. They should be free from unrighteousness, but they're free from righteousness, free from holiness, free from godliness, free from the sinless life. They are candidates for the pits of hell and the lake of fire. Ask yourself the question: *Am I free from righteousness?* Then consider: *If I were free from sin, I would have righteousness in me.*

This is good study; drink it in, let it become a part of you. Know the scriptures, for in them you have eternal life.

ARE YOU PROUD OF YOUR SINS?

What fruit had ye then in those things whereof ye are now ashamed? for the end of those things is death (Romans 6:21). We're ashamed; we don't want to talk about the sins we've committed. We'll tell enough to help people, but we don't glory in them or have ego about them. I've heard people and even preachers talk who had much ego over the sins they used to commit. They ought to be ashamed of those sins! God is ashamed that you committed them; and, for you to have godly sorrow, you have to be as ashamed of those sins as God is; then you can receive forgiveness.

When you're not free from sin, you're free from righteousness. Those preachers who preach that everybody sins are not free from sin, so they are not righteous. Why would you want to keep talking about your sins as though they're big and wonderful?

Ashamed of your sins, you're telling them for the glory of God to warn others not to fall into the same trap you were in. Paul confessed that he was the chief of sinners, didn't he? **This is a faithful saying, and worthy of all acceptation, that Christ Jesus came into the world to save sinners; of whom I am chief** (I Timothy 1:15).

But now being made free from sin, and become servants to God, ye have your fruit unto holiness, and the end everlasting life (Romans 6:22). You can't be a servant of God until you're free from sin. God has righteous servants only. You must be careful to be obedient in everything the Lord wants you to do; put Him first, and that you will do as long as He is your first love.

When you were saved you did only that which pleased the Lord; in fact, you didn't want to do anything that wouldn't please Him. As long as you kept that first love, you were all right.

For the wages of sin is death; but the gift of God is eternal life through Jesus Christ our Lord (Romans 6:23). When Adam and Eve committed one sin, the wage was damnation, death; they lost everything. They were cast out of their heaven on earth, cast into sin and the clutches of the devil. They saw the Lord turn His back on them and walk away. My God!

So many people have nothing but the back of God, that's all. He will never look their way again because of how they have treated Him, how they have misused His holy Word, and how they have brought damnation on themselves by blaspheming the Gospel. They have committed crimes against God, and God's Spirit has lifted from them.

SERVE IN THE NEWNESS OF THE SPIRIT

Wherefore, my brethren, ye also are become dead to the law by the body of Christ; that ye should be married to another, even to him who is raised from the dead, that we should bring forth fruit unto God (Romans 7:4). This is rich. Jesus was the fulfillment of the Law, and this verse plainly tells us we should be married to Him. Some people claim that Jerusalem is the Bride of Christ. Who would marry a city? This verse tells us that Christ is married to the Church; it says nothing about the New Jerusalem. We're not married to the Law, not obligated to the Law; we're obligated to grace.

For when we were in the flesh, the motions of sins, which were by the law, did work in our members to bring forth fruit unto death (Romans 7:5). The Law couldn't bring the born again experience; only grace can do that, the grace blood.

But now we are delivered from the law, that be-

ing dead wherein we were held; that we should serve in newness of spirit, and not in the oldness of the letter** (Romans 7:6). The Law is the oldness of the letter, but we serve in the newness of the Spirit through the Gospel.

What shall we say then? Is the law sin? God forbid. Nay, I had not known sin, but by the law: for I had not known lust, except the law had said, Thou shalt not covet. For I was alive without the law once: but when the commandment came, sin revived, and I died. And the commandment, which was ordained to life, I found to be unto death. For sin, taking occasion by the commandment, deceived me, and by it slew me (Romans 7:7,9–11). The commandment was judgment, death according to the Law and no mercy. And this is where many preachers get into false doctrine: They say that Paul admitted he never was free from sin, that he had to sin; however, Paul never said any such thing. In these verses in Romans 7, he was talking about being under the Law and how the Law affected him. What the Law didn't do for him and what the Law couldn't accomplish, grace did.

Wherefore the law is holy, and the commandment holy, and just, and good (Romans 7:12). That is because it came from God, but man wouldn't obey it and live up to it. Man couldn't keep the Ten Commandments without divine blood; it was impossible. Man didn't have the love of God in him to do it or to keep everything God said.

PAUL UNDER THE LAW

Was then that which is good made death unto me? God forbid. But sin, that it might appear sin, working death in me by that which is good; that sin by the commandment might become exceeding sinful (Romans 7:13). Paul learned much as he looked back on his life. The Holy Spirit taught him why his emotions were what they were, and why, after the Day of Atonement once a year, that his nation went back into sin.

For we know that the law is spiritual: but I am carnal, sold under sin (Romans 7:14). This was Paul's condition under the Law. He's describing what he was under the Law.

For that which I do I allow not: for what I would, that do I not; but what I hate, that do I (Romans 7:15). Do you see how complicated the Law was? Salvation isn't complicated; you're either saved and free from all sin, or you belong to the devil.

Paul is describing the confusion he had under the Law. The Lord isn't the author of confusion, and this is confusion. **For God is not the author of confusion, but of peace, as in all churches of the** saints (I Corinthians 14:33).

Preacher, that confuses me, too!

Paul was being frank to let people know what it was like being under the Law.

If then I do that which I would not, I consent unto the law that it is good. Now then it is no more I that do it, but sin that dwelleth in me (Romans 7: 16,17). Sin can't work within us if we are to please God and go to heaven.

For I know that in me (that is, in my flesh,) dwelleth no good thing (Romans 7:18). Again, this was when Paul was under the Law and no good thing dwelt in him. He was a strict Pharisee; and, he confessed, a chief of sinners.

For to will is present with me; but how to perform that which is good I find not (Romans 7:18). Paul wasn't persecuted when he was a Pharisee and keeping the Law; he was just lost.

For the good that I would I do not: but the evil which I would not, that I do (Romans 7:19). Paul is talking about a Law person here and not a grace person. He's describing what the Law couldn't do. Moses gave the Law, but Jesus came and brought grace and truth. **For the law was given by Moses, but grace and truth came by Jesus Christ** (John 1:17).

Now if I do that I would not, it is no more I that

do it, but sin that dwelleth in me. I find then a law, that, when I would do good, evil is present with me (Romans 7:20,21). The Law hadn't worked for Paul, and he's telling this to the Romans who were still trying to hold onto Law. Jesus had brought love-law, and it's through love that Paul now served the Lord.

In the thirteenth chapter of first Corinthians, Paul gives the definition of divine love. He talks a lot about the love in which we must be rooted and grounded. **That Christ may dwell in your hearts by faith; that ye, being rooted and grounded in love, May be able to comprehend with all saints what is the breadth, and length, and depth, and height; And to know the love of Christ, which passeth knowledge** (Ephesians 3:17–19).

THE LAW CAN'T SAVE US FROM SIN

For I delight in the law of God after the inward man: But I see another law in my members, warring against the law of my mind, and bringing me into captivity to the law of sin which is in my members (Romans 7:22,23). The Law couldn't keep Paul from sinning. Once a year on the Day of Atonement, the high priest could enter that most holy place in the temple and meet God at the mercy seat. Everyone else had to stand outside. Were the high priest to die while he was in the most high place, no one could go in to bring him out; it meant death for anyone who would try. A rope was tied around the priest in case he had to be dragged out; and, as he ministered before the Lord, bells on his garment would jingle to let others know he was still alive and moving.

If some of these "dead" preachers today were Old Testament priests, they would have to be dragged out because they won't minister in the holiness of God. I've often thought of that.

O wretched man that I am (Romans 7:24)! After Paul was saved, he wasn't a wretched man. He said, **Rejoice in the Lord alway: and again I say, Rejoice** (Philippians 4:4). **For I have learned, in whatsoever state I am, therewith to be content** (Philippians 4:11). How could a person be wretched and still be content? No scripture is of a private interpretation; always keep that in mind when you're studying the Word of God. **Knowing this first, that no prophecy of the scripture is of any private interpretation** (II Peter 1:20).

Paul was talking about himself, what it was like when he walked after the flesh and wasn't free from sin. He wanted to do good at times. Didn't you want to do good sometimes when you were a child, especially when you were told you would get something special if you did? Then you would fool and deceive your parents because you really hadn't been that good.

Who shall deliver me from the body of this death? I thank God through Jesus Christ our Lord (Romans 7:24,25). This is the answer in one statement. Paul was delivered when he met Jesus on the road to Damascus. **And Saul** [Paul], **yet breathing out threatenings and slaughter against the disciples of the Lord, went unto the high priest, And desired of him letters to Damascus to the synagogues, that if he found any of this way, whether they were men or women, he might bring them bound unto Jerusalem. And as he journeyed, he came near Damascus: and suddenly there shined round about him a light from heaven: And he fell to the earth, and heard a voice saying unto him, Saul, Saul, why persecutest thou me? And he said, Who art thou, Lord? And the Lord said, I am Jesus whom thou persecutest: it is hard for thee to kick against the pricks** (Acts 9:1–5). *"I am Jesus,"* the Lord told Saul. *"I am grace; I am deliverance; I am salvation; I am heaven. Accept the Gospel that I brought!"* And that Paul did.

There is therefore now no condemnation to them which are in Christ Jesus, who walk not after the

flesh, but after the Spirit (Romans 8:1).

For the law of the Spirit of life in Christ Jesus hath made me free from the law of sin and death (Romans 8:2). Eternal death means the soul that sinneth shall die. Paul said Jesus made him free from death; he had life, eternal life. **This is the covenant that I will make with them after those days, saith the Lord, I will put my laws into their hearts, and in their minds will I write them; And their sins and iniquities will I remember no more** (Hebrews 10:16,17).

When you get saved, you're given eternal life. Jesus told Nicodemus, **Ye must be born again** (John 3:7). Nicodemus didn't understand it. He was supposed to be a noted teacher of the Jews, but being born again was a foreign language to him; it was grace. The teachers in that day didn't know about grace; they just knew about and taught the Law.

For what the law could not do, in that it was weak through the flesh, God sending his own Son in the likeness of sinful flesh, and for sin, condemned sin in the flesh (Romans 8:3). If you do what God condemns, you're condemned automatically; that's the Word of God.

NOT ALL CAN ENTER THROUGH THE GATE

This is powerful and as deep as God Himself.

Anyone who tries to get around the Word is trying to get around God the Father, God the Son, God the Holy Ghost, and all the righteous angels. The Lord plainly tells you that, although He lets people come outside the gate, not all can go in. Read in Revelation the kind of people who will be standing outside, denied. **For without are dogs, and sorcerers, and whoremongers, and murderers, and idolaters, and whosoever loveth and maketh a lie** (Revelation 22:15).

That the righteousness of the law might be fulfilled in us, who walk not after the flesh, but after the Spirit (Romans 8:4). The righteousness of the law that Christ brought is the law of love and grace, not the Mosaic Law. Paul said it was impossible to walk after the Spirit through the Law of Moses.

For they that are after the flesh do mind the things of the flesh (Romans 8:5). Many Christians in this final hour will fail God because they want to please the flesh. Think about what Paul said of Demas: **For Demas hath forsaken me, having loved this present world** (II Timothy 4:10). What a teacher, what a friend, what a light Demas once had in the apostle Paul! Demas could have been in heaven forever, but he's been in hell a couple thousand years now; and he'll never get out. My God!

But they that are after the Spirit [mind] **the**

things of the Spirit (Romans 8:5). When you have grace, you follow the things of the Spirit. But when you don't have grace, you consider what the flesh wants and not what God wants. You don't come out of bed each morning wanting the will of God in everything; you want your own way. **There is a way which seemeth right unto a man, but the end thereof are the ways of death** (Proverbs 14:12). **Wherefore come out from among them, and be ye separate, saith the Lord, and touch not the unclean thing; and I will receive you** (II Corinthians 6:17).

It seems right to some so-called Christians to mind the flesh; you can tell they're in the flesh by their conversation, by the way they treat God, His Word, and His services.

THE CARNAL MIND IS AN ENEMY OF GOD

For to be carnally minded is death (Romans 8:6). To have a worldly mind is death.

But to be spiritually minded is life and peace (Romans 8:6). You have life; you have peace when you're born again. Enjoy the abundant life He brought. **I am come that they might have life, and that they might have it more abundantly** (John 10:10). Don't wait until you get to heaven to enjoy abundant life, and don't let the devil make you doubt it; enjoy it now. Abundant life is holy. It gives you strength to go forward, operates your mind in a beautiful fashion to understand what God wants you to know. It gives you the ability to be able to reason with God and to have the mind of Christ.

Because the carnal mind is enmity against God: for it is not subject to the law of God, neither indeed can be (Romans 8:7). The carnal mind is not subject to the law of God's love. One must have the right mind, the mind of Jesus, to really yield to and use the love of God.

So then they that are in the flesh cannot please God (Romans 8:8). Can you *not* please God and go to heaven? No, you'll go to hell. You have to please God.

But ye are not in the flesh, but in the Spirit, if so be that the Spirit of God dwell in you. Now if any man have not the Spirit of Christ, he is none of his (Romans 8:9). If you don't have the Spirit of Christ in you, the Spirit of holiness and righteousness, you're not a child of God.

And if Christ be in you, the body is dead because of sin (Romans 8:10). The body is dead to sin when Christ is in you. Paul said, **I am crucified with Christ: nevertheless I live; yet not I, but Christ liveth in me** (Galatians 2:20). We have Christ; He lives in us.

QUICKENED BY THE HOLY SPIRIT

But the Spirit is life because of righteousness (Romans 8:10). The Holy Spirit is the life of heaven in you; He operates with divine life. In your prayer time and Bible study, He gives you life and the Spirit of life to reason with your Maker, life to listen to and hear what the Spirit is saying. He gives life to your eyes to see that which is spiritual, that which is right, that which is wonderful and pleasing to God.

The tongue? The blood took all the deceit out when you got saved. If you stay saved, that deceit will not be there; but, if you become backslidden, that deceit will take over. When those spirits take you over again, you become worse than you ever were before you got saved; the Bible declares it. **When the unclean spirit is gone out of a man, he walketh through dry places, seeking rest, and findeth none. Then he saith, I will return into my house from whence I came out; and when he is come, he findeth it empty, swept, and garnished. Then goeth he, and taketh with himself seven other spirits more wicked than himself, and they enter in and dwell there: and the last state of that man is worse than the first** (Matthew 12:43–45).

But if the Spirit of him that raised up Jesus from the dead dwell in you, he that raised up Christ from the dead shall also quicken your mortal bodies by his Spirit [the Holy Spirit] **that dwelleth in you** (Romans 8:11). Quicken means to enliven. The Holy Spirit enlivens your body so you are able to give over to Him. The Holy Spirit doesn't have any problems with you, and you don't grieve Him. You make Him laugh and rejoice; you're a pleasure to Him. Take His discipline. Use God's theories and not your own; use the thoughts of God.

When the Holy Spirit dwells in you, He will be your teacher, your guide, the Spirit of truth. Jesus told the disciples, **And I will pray the Father, and he shall give you another Comforter, that he may abide with you for ever; Even the Spirit of truth; whom the world cannot receive, because it seeth him not, neither knoweth him: but ye know him; for he dwelleth with you, and shall be in you** (John 14:16,17).

Therefore, brethren, we are debtors, not to the flesh, to live after the flesh (Romans 8:12). We don't owe the flesh anything; we owe everything to the Spirit, everything to God. We owe our lives to God, to live after the Spirit. **For if ye live after the flesh, ye shall die** [an eternal death]**: but if ye through the Spirit do mortify the deeds of the body, ye shall live** (Romans 8:13).

Those who cater to the flesh, live after the flesh, and soothe the flesh, are not willing to sacrifice for the Spirit. However, the Bible says that **if we suffer, we shall also reign with him** (II Timothy 2:12).

For as many as are led by the Spirit of God, they are the sons [or daughters] **of God** (Romans 8:14). You're not a son or daughter of God if you're not led by the Spirit. When the flesh is leading you, it means the spirit of the devil is leading you.

For ye have not received the spirit of bondage again to fear (Romans 8:15). Sin and disobedience are bondage, but we who have Jesus have nothing to fear and nothing to worry about. No ungodly fear is ours and no fear of judgment is held over our heads.

But ye have received the Spirit of adoption, whereby we cry, Abba, Father (Romans 8:15). The Lord is our Father. Jesus taught the disciples in the Sermon on the Mount to pray, **Our Father which art in heaven, Hallowed be thy name. Thy kingdom come. Thy will be done in earth, as it is in heaven** (Matthew 6:9,10). We are to pray for God's Kingdom to hurry and come. Many people don't realize that Jesus is speaking of the Perfect Age in that prayer. God's will won't be done on the earth until the thousand-year reign of Christ when He sets up His Kingdom of righteousness. We can pray until our tongues fall out, but it won't happen until the thousand years come, the Perfect Age.

JOINT-HEIRS WITH CHRIST

The [Holy] Spirit itself beareth witness with our spirit, that we are the children of God (Romans 8:16). You should make sure that the Holy Spirit bears witness at all times with your spirit. Don't go to sleep without knowing that you've committed no willful sin, no willful disobedience against God, but knowing that you have pleased Him.

And if children, then heirs; heirs of God, and joint-heirs with Christ (Romans 8:17). Do you think the Lord would make somebody with a seed of sin in his or her life a joint-heir with His only begotten Son?—Not so.

If so be that we suffer with him, that we may be also glorified together (Romans 8:17). We suffer because of sin in the world, and those who disobey will suffer also.

For I reckon that the sufferings of this present time are not worthy to be compared with the glory which shall be revealed in us (Romans 8:18). Sorrows causing many tears are magnified in us now; but, on tomorrow, the Lord will magnify His glory in us. It will all be glory with no sorrows and no tears. With His love handkerchief, Jehovah God will wipe away all tears. Then He'll wipe away the tears from the eyes of His Son and the Holy Ghost. At last, with that great love, He'll take His love handkerchief and wipe away His tears to never cry over another lost soul. He'll shut them away from His memory; He told me He would do it. He has the power to do it, and He will do it.

For the earnest expectation of the creature waiteth for the manifestation of the sons of God. For the creature was made subject to vanity, not willingly, but by reason of him who hath subjected the same in hope, Because the creature itself also shall be delivered from the bondage of corruption into the glorious liberty of the children of God (Romans 8:19–21). This is talking about the animals being delivered in the Perfect Age. The lion, the bear and all beasts will be tame. There will be no evil or wild beasts.

For we know that the whole creation groaneth and travaileth in pain together until now (Romans 8:22). Think what the animals suffer, what they go through. And many of them also live in fear of their lives.

And not only they, but ourselves also, which have the firstfruits of the Spirit, even we ourselves groan within ourselves, waiting for the adoption, to wit, the redemption of our body (Romans 8:23). We do sigh for the new body, especially when we're in great pain. Children of God become willing to die to get out of the old house and to leave it behind.

They become willing to leave behind those whom they've loved for years and never thought they'd ever be willing to leave. They become willing because of the condition their body is in. That's what Paul is talking about, not only do the animals groan, but we also groan.

DIVINE HOPE

For we are saved by hope: but hope that is seen is not hope: for what a man seeth, why doth he yet hope for? But if we hope for that we see not, then do we with patience wait for it (Romans 8:24,25). We hope for that new body with divine hope; and, because of the divine hope, we know it's coming. We know it will happen. We'll have our new body without an ache, a pain, or any sickness. The time will come when there will be no sickness, no hospitals, no doctors, and no cemeteries; there will only be heaven, beautiful heaven.

Likewise the Spirit also helpeth our infirmities: for we know not what we should pray for as we ought: but the Spirit [the Holy Ghost] **itself maketh intercession for us with groanings which cannot be uttered** (Romans 8:26). Many of you have had the Holy Ghost cry through you; I've heard it again and again. I've come to that place many, many times when I couldn't express in words what

I felt, and the Holy Ghost would groan through me with great power and grace. I would listen to the groanings and find much comfort knowing He was making intercession for me.

Don't let the groanings of the Holy Spirit depress you; they're blessed, and they bring blessed results. It's been proven in this work time and time again when, even after hours and hours of looking to God, the answer hadn't yet come. The Holy Ghost makes intercession because He knows the will of God, and I leave everything to the will of God. I have a standing order in heaven for God to never answer a prayer I pray unless it is His divine will.

And he that searcheth the hearts knoweth what is the mind of the Spirit, because he maketh intercession for the saints according to the will of God (Romans 8:27). God searches the heart; the Spirit knows if you're yielded to the Father's will. The Holy Spirit makes intercession for the saints of God only according to the will of God; remember that. You have the Holy Spirit, your teacher, your guide; and He will make intercession for you only if you want the will of God. But if you don't want God's will, forget it; you're on your own.

And we know that all things work together for good to them that love God, to them who are the called according to his purpose (Romans 8:28).

Remember, all things work for good to them who love God; they work with divine love for people who are doing His will, being obedient, pleasing Him in everything. They are not doing what they have chosen to do but rather what God has called them to do. They know they have God's calling; and, if they don't obey, their ugly disobedience will separate them from their God and the Holy Spirit. Disobedience causes the Holy Spirit to take His flight, and the Holy Spirit can move out faster than He came in.

Knowing that all things work together for good to them that are the called according to His purpose, you pray in perfect faith with no room for doubt. God has a purpose in His great plan for each one of you in this final hour just as He had a purpose for every member of Noah's righteous family. Today we are the righteous family of God, obedient to Him.

GOD KNEW PEOPLE WOULD ANSWER HIS CALL

For whom he did foreknow, he also did predestinate to be conformed to the image of his Son, that he might be the firstborn among many brethren (Romans 8:29). The Lord foreknew there would be a people who would become His people, holy and righteous, accepting the divine blood.

Moreover whom he did predestinate, them he

also called: and whom he called, them he also justified: and whom he justified, them he also glorified (Romans 8:30). God predestinated people who would be called, who would answer the call. He called you who would be justified in answering His call. And whom He justified He also would glorify, finding no fault, no condemnation in them.

When you're holy in the eyes of God and free from all sin, you're already glorified before Him. When God looks at you through the blood and sees His own image, His Son's and the Holy Spirit's image, He sees glorification.

These are thoughts that the Lord gives; let Him give you even more thoughts. This last hour is the hour of great revelation. The Lord tells us again and again: *This is your hour of revelation, your hour of visitation.* So don't say you don't understand; study to show yourself approved, a workman that needeth not to be ashamed, rightly dividing the Word of truth.

What shall we then say to these things? If God be for us, who can be against us (Romans 8:31)? If God is for you, no matter how many devils come against you, you're more than a conqueror; you have nothing to be afraid of. Through the blood you have power to conquer all devils that come after you and power left over for any more devils that may come, so you live with full assurance that everything will be all right.

He that spared not his own Son, but delivered him up for us all, how shall he not with him also freely give us all things (Romans 8:32)? The Lord will give all things needed. Since God delivered up His beloved Son, His very heart and only begotten who died for all, why would He not also freely give us all things, spiritually, physically and financially? **Trust in the LORD with all thine heart; and lean not unto thine own understanding. In all thy ways acknowledge him, and he shall direct thy paths** (Proverbs 3:5,6).

Who shall lay any thing to the charge of God's elect? It is God that justifieth (Romans 8:33). Had Jesus paid attention to people who came against Him, He never would have delivered the plan of redemption and never would have made it to the Cross. Jesus said to beware of anyone that all men speak well of; they're hypocrites; they have many faces. **Woe unto you, when all men shall speak well of you! for so did their fathers to the false prophets** (Luke 6:26).

But these are not of the world, Jesus said of the disciples with Him. **They are not of the world, even as I am not of the world. Neither pray I for these alone, but for them also which shall believe**

on me through their word (John 17:14,20). Jesus prayed for us, too.

JESUS MAKES INTERCESSION

Who is he that condemneth? It is Christ that died, yea rather, that is risen again, who is even at the right hand of God, who also maketh intercession for us (Romans 8:34). Nobody else but Jesus has a right to condemn us; He alone died for us. Jesus is at the right hand of the Father today making intercession for each one of you who is in the will of God. If you're not in the will of God, your only hope is pleading for forgiveness with godly sorrow that worketh repentance unto salvation. **For godly sorrow worketh repentance to salvation not to be repented of** (II Corinthians 7:10). *Your prayers get nowhere unless you measure up to this verse, saith the Lord.* They go only as far as your physical voice will carry them, and then they bounce back—how sad!

In the eighth chapter of Romans, you learn that you have both the Holy Spirit and Jesus to intercede to the Father for you. The devil can do nothing with the blood-line that Jesus put up. When you pray, *Father, in the name of Jesus I come,* it means you come in His holiness, His righteousness, His love, His faith, His obedience, His humility; you come in

His everything. The Lord hears that voice. Jesus said, *Father, you always hear me!* **Father, I thank thee that thou hast heard me. And I knew that thou hearest me always** (John 11:41,42).

Do you see why the truth about living free from sin has to go forth? You need to study it because it will give you the anointing to understand it in a great way—*if you take the anointing, saith the Lord.* The Lord gave me the revelation that those who hear it (or read it) will get a special anointing of understanding that goes out through the Holy Spirit, through the Lord speaking through me.

SAFE IN CHRIST'S LOVE

Who shall separate us from the love of Christ? shall tribulation, or distress, or persecution, or famine, or nakedness, or peril, or sword? As it is written, For thy sake we are killed all the day long; we are accounted as sheep for the slaughter (Romans 8:35,36). The early Christians didn't know at what time they might be killed, when they might be arrested and put to death for the sake of Christ. But some preachers have taught—and really believed—that Paul meant we couldn't be sanctified and made holy once and for all, that he was saying we had to be sanctified anew daily, die daily to self. Why, that's as good as any lie the devil wants you to believe, next to believing you can't live free from sin. That's ridiculous! Paul didn't die daily; he gave everything to the Lord, and proved it. He went forth into the wilderness for nearly three-and-a-half years to be taught by the Holy Ghost.

Sanctification isn't something you gradually come into. To sanctify means to make holy. **Sanctify them through thy truth: thy word is truth** (John 17:17). A lot of people think salvation comes by degrees.

I remember a story about a little boy who didn't want to hurt his dog, but he wanted him to have a bobbed tail. He cut the dog's tail off a little bit at a time because he thought it wouldn't hurt as much. It's not like that with God; He so loved you that He gave Jesus, a one-time gift. Jesus doesn't have to be crucified day after day in your life for you to be sanctified. You had better believe that and quit all your sinning. I quit all of mine, took on the Spirit of the Lord, and started preaching His Gospel.

Nay, in all these things we are more than conquerors through him that loved us (Romans 8:37). You conquer through Jesus' blood-love. Without His love you're nothing, just an empty shell. But through His love, in all these things we are more than conquerors; we have nothing to fear, nothing to worry about. That's great, isn't it?

For I am persuaded [I have full assurance]**, that neither death, nor life, nor angels, nor principalities, nor powers, nor things present, nor things to come, Nor height, nor depth, nor any other creature, shall be able to separate us from the love of God, which is in Christ Jesus our Lord** (Romans 8:38,39). That is the love in Christ Jesus.

PAUL PREACHED GRACE

What shall we say then? That the Gentiles, which followed not after righteousness, have attained to righteousness, even the righteousness which is of faith. But Israel, which followed after the law of righteousness, hath not attained to the law of righteousness. Wherefore? Because they sought it not by faith, but as it were by the works of the law. For they stumbled at that stumblingstone; As it is written, Behold, I lay in Sion a stumblingstone and rock of offence: and whosoever believeth on him shall not be ashamed (Romans 9:30–33). Paul didn't spare the ones he preached the Gospel to. He didn't preach the Law, he preached grace; and they came to the Lord justified. But to the Jews who did not accept the Gospel, Paul told them that they were not justified in the eyes of God. They were left out, for they let Christ become a stumbling block, a rock of offense.

Chapter 10: Some Final Words To The Romans

John the Baptist asked Jesus the question, **Art thou he that should come? or look we for another** (Luke 7:19)? And Jesus sent this message back to him, **Blessed is he, whosoever shall not be offended in me** (Luke 7:23). Aren't you glad that you are not offended or ashamed of His Gospel?

Brethren, my heart's desire and prayer to God for Israel is, that they might be saved. For I bear them record that they have a zeal of God, but not according to knowledge (Romans 10:1,2). The devil has zeal; people can have zeal without any God connected to it at all.

For they being ignorant of God's righteousness, and going about to establish their own righteousness, have not submitted themselves unto the righteousness of God (Romans 10:3). Many preachers have established their own righteousness, and they have no righteousness of God. You have to submit to the righteousness of God to have it.

For Christ is the end of the law for righteousness to every one that believeth (Romans 10:4). Christ is the end of the Law, the Law of Moses. Jesus came to fulfill the Law, not to destroy it. Righteousness and grace came through Jesus Christ.

For Moses describeth the righteousness which is of the law, That the man which doeth those things shall live by them. But the righteousness

which is of faith speaketh on this wise, Say not in thine heart, Who shall ascend into heaven? (that is, to bring Christ down from above:) Or, Who shall descend into the deep? (that is, to bring up Christ again from the dead.) But what saith it? The word is nigh thee, even in thy mouth, and in thy heart: that is, the word of faith, which we preach** (Romans 10:5–8). Keep in mind that Paul is still separating Law and grace: Law to the left, and grace to the right.

JESUS IS OUR ONLY SALVATION

That if thou shalt confess with thy mouth the Lord Jesus [and many of the Jews would not do it], **and shalt believe in thine heart that God hath raised him from the dead,** [then and then only] **thou shalt be saved** (Romans 10:9). The Bible also tells us, **Neither is there salvation in any other: for there is none other name under heaven given among men, whereby we must be saved** (Acts 4:12). Neither false religions nor the Law will bring salvation; it only comes through Christ, and He brought grace for all.

For with the heart man believeth unto righteousness; and with the mouth confession is made unto salvation (Romans 10:10). You have to have righteousness in your heart before you make the true confession of salvation.

Truth has to be established in the heart first and foremost, and many people don't realize this. It doesn't first come into the mind or the mouth; truth has to enter the heart and take it over.

For the scripture saith, Whosoever believeth on him shall not be ashamed. For there is no difference between the Jew and the Greek: for the same Lord over all is rich unto all that call upon him (Romans 10:11,12). It doesn't matter what nationality you are, God is for you. He's for the Jews, and He's for those Gentiles who have been adopted into the family of God.

For whosoever shall call upon the name of the Lord shall be saved (Romans 10:13). How simple it is when truth goes into hearts. That's what happens in our great crusades overseas; the truth goes into hearts. The Lord showed me through the divine blood truth that truth and the divine blood bring devils under submission. The divine blood helps people give their minds over to the Gospel that has been preached so they can accept it, often in that same service. Then, as they submit their minds, they yield to the divine blood. The blood drops into their souls and the devils go out; now the people are ready to receive Jesus Christ.

All we have to do is preach the true Gospel and live

so the light will shine through us. Jesus said we are His lights to light up the world. **Ye are the light of the world ... Let your light so shine before men, that they may see your good works, and glorify your Father which is in heaven** (Matthew 5:14,16). He is the great light, and *that light shineth, saith the Lord.* But we are the reflectors of His light.

Let the light shine through you; seek day and night for it to always shine. Don't miss a soul; don't do anything that would hinder someone from coming to the Lord. Have patience with people in finding the Lord.

The Lord gives me compassion for the people when He tells me they're in ignorance, that the preachers are in ignorance, and that He has sent me to help them in love. The Lord shows great love. He's told me to tell others how much He hates witchcraft and that they'll go to hell for it; but He loves them, and He's sent us to help deliver them. They can be free. People don't have to fear witchcraft, voodoo or any darknesses of the devil, not even the devil himself. God has all power, and He wants people to know it.

Thus saith the Lord: I am here, loving you with an unending love, loving you with the voice of heaven and the greatness of heaven. My eyes are upon you to do you good, saith the Lord, and

I am never afar off; I'm always nigh. My divine blood makes you [so] nigh unto me that you can appear before my holy throne any time while you're still on earth.

My Spirit prayeth for thee, and I am listening. My Spirit is calling for you to receive more help, you that are sincere before the Lord your God, and He's calling for more help. Open your hearts now to my Spirit, saith the Lord, and my Spirit will flow this great anointing in to give you that help that you need to bring in more lost humanity, and to give you more wisdom and more knowledge.

Remember, man and woman lost heaven (Eden) all because of one sin. *The soul that sinneth shall die!* Child of God, you must never go back to the tree of death. The tree of life (Jesus) is yours. He and He alone is your passport to heaven.

About the Author

Reverend Ernest Angley, pastor and founder of Ernest Angley's Grace Cathedral in Akron, Ohio, is in the midst of a tremendous worldwide outreach, spreading the Gospel by way of crusades, television and the printed page into many nations. God has endowed Reverend Angley with special gifts to bring healing for soul, mind and body to the multitudes. He does not claim to be a healer, but a witness to the marvelous healing power of Christ. His television programs, "The Ernest Angley Hour" (aired weekly) and "The Ninety and Nine Club" (aired daily), present the fullness of God's Word to the people—salvation, healing and the baptism in the Holy Ghost.

Check your local listing for times in your area.

You Are Special To God

Visit our website at www.ernestangley.org

MORE BOOKS
by Ernest Angley

RAPTURED
$3.50
A novel by Ernest Angley about the second coming of Christ based on biblical facts. This timely book could change your life.

FAITH IN GOD HEALS THE SICK
$1.95
An instructive book by Ernest Angley telling not only how to receive physical healing from the Lord, but also how to keep that healing.

UNTYING GOD'S HANDS
$10.00   (NEW EDITION — FULL SIZE)
With amazing frankness the author has dealt with many controversial subjects in this book: the ministry of angels, preparation required for the Rapture, guidelines for dating, sex in marriage, sex outside marriage, masturbation, homosexuality. Many other subjects covering the whole life of man are woven into the underlying theme of how to untie God's hands.

CELL 15
$2.95
The dramatic true story of the imprisonment of Reverend Ernest Angley in Munich, Germany, for preaching the Gospel and praying for the sick.

GOD'S RAINBOW OF PROMISES
$1.95

Precious promises from the Word of God (KJV) to cover your every need now and forever will enhance your personal devotions and prove a great blessing in time of trouble.

THE DECEIT OF LUCIFER
$10.00

Using the Word of God as the only standard, Reverend Angley strips the camouflage of Lucifer's insidious deceit from demonology, seducing spirits and the counterfeit works of God. A culmination of information derived from years of training by the Holy Spirit, this book is a must for anyone who wishes to recognize the deadly pitfalls of the dangerous endtime hour in which we live.

LEECHING OF THE MIND
$10.00

Like parasitic leeches of the jungle that live off the blood of their victims, leeches of the mind sap the life force of reason. Through the gifts of the Holy Spirit, Reverend Angley exposes the inner working of Lucifer in the human mind, revealing the most incredible takeover by Lucifer a person could suffer other than total devil possession of the soul.

THE POWER OF BIBLE FASTING
$10.00

The Power Of Bible Fasting is one of the most thorough books on Bible fasting ever written, an invaluable guide into a deeper walk with God and the reality of His presence.

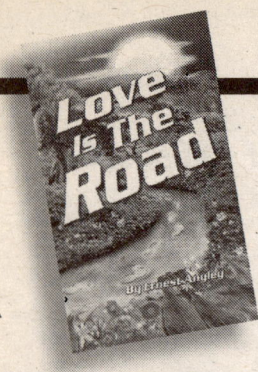

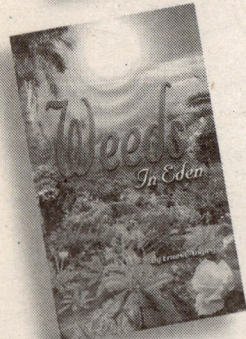

LOVE IS THE ROAD
$10.00

Through His great and precious promises we receive much from the Lord on His Love Road. The Love Road is a supernatural Road laid out by supernatural power, planned by the Lord God Almighty. Discover how you, too, can walk this marvelous Road into the fullness and greatness of God in this last and final hour.

WEEDS IN EDEN
$10.00

One of God's greatest disappointments: Finding weeds in Eden. *Weeds in Eden* describes the cost to God and man of minds overrun with the weeds of disobedience and rebellion. The price paid by heaven and earth was sorrow, heartache and despair, and the price today is still the same. Let this book help you search out any weeds that would contaminate the Eden of your mind in this last and final hour.

THE UNFORGIVABLE SIN
$10.00

There is a sin not even Calvary can pardon. Once people commit this sin, only doom and damnation await them with no chance ever of heaven. Jesus said, *All manner of sin and blasphemy shall be forgiven unto men, but the blasphemy against the Holy Ghost shall not be forgiven unto men . . . neither in this world, neither in the world to come* (Matthew 12:31, 32)

REALITY OF THE BLOOD: VOL. 1
$10.00

In this enlightened book on divine blood, the unique and insightful author, through the power of the Holy Ghost, opens up amazing revelations about the importance of the blood of Jesus for all people. Those who love God with all their heart will be thrilled to find the marvelous understanding of the blood that has been set down in this book.

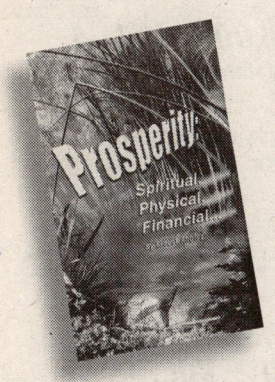

PROSPERITY: SPIRITUAL, PHYSICAL, FINANCIAL...
$10.00
To bring forth the fullness of God's prosperity that we find in His divine will, the writer has gone into the deepness of the Holy Spirit and the Word of God. Prosperity for soul, mind and body is God's will for all His Children.

REALITY OF THE BLOOD: VOL. 2
**They used the Blood . . .
We must use the Blood**
$10.00
The power in the divine blood of Jesus is being presented in living reality as multitudes experience miracles of healing for soul, mind and body. The Early Church used divine blood through the power of the Holy Ghost, now it's time for the Church in this last and final hour to use the power in the divine blood.

REALITY OF THE BLOOD: VOL. 3
Faith and Feelings!
$10.00
Through the Spirit of God recognize the difference between feelings and faith. Feelings can dishearten you if you rely on them to determine your benefits with God and what you should do for Him. Trusting in feelings is the reason so many Christians have battles of the mind.

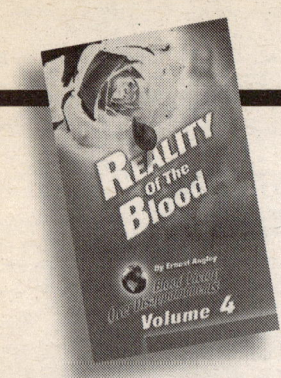

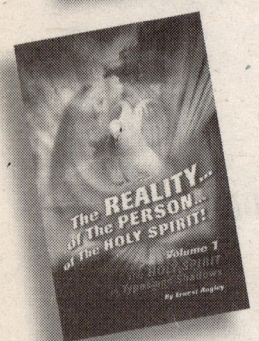

REALITY OF THE BLOOD: VOL. 4
Blood Victory Over Disappointments!
$10.00
Realize what is yours through divine blood: freedom from depression, oppression, sin, sickness, disease and all other bondages of the devil. Through divine blood it is possible to overcome Satan's great weapon of disappointments and take on the mind of Jesus.

THE REALITY OF THE PERSON OF THE HOLY SPIRIT: VOL. 1
The Holy Spirit in Types and Shadows
$10.00
Reverend Angley lifts the mist curtains of the Old Testament to reveal the Holy Spirit in types and shadows. Let these marvelous types and shadows come alive in your heart and thrill your very being.

THE REALITY OF THE PERSON OF THE HOLY SPIRIT: VOL. 2
The Holy Spirit and Fire
$10.00
The fire of the Holy Spirit includes great miracles of deliverance as well as the devouring fire of judgment. Read how the fire of the Holy Spirit will affect your life.

THE REALITY OF THE PERSON OF THE HOLY SPIRIT: VOL. 3
The Holy Spirit in the New and Old Testaments
$10.00
The Holy Spirit worked throughout the New Testament, but did He work in Old Testament days? Yes, He did. Read about it in volume 3 of the Holy Spirit series.

HURRY FRIDAY!
Autobiography of Ernest Angley: Elegant Hardcover Edition
$30.00

Hurry Friday! will make you laugh, cry, and rejoice in the amazing way God has moved in the life of this unique servant of God.

THE MIND OF CHRIST
$10.00

Let this mind be in you, which was also in Christ (Philippians 2:5). What made up His mind? Listed in this book are 141 ingredients found in the mind of Christ.

THE REALITY OF THE PERSON OF THE HOLY SPIRIT: VOL. 4
The Mantle of Power
$10.00

The Bible is filled with examples of the Holy Ghost using the mantle of power through godly men and women. All the truth of God as well as His power is in the mantle. Recognize the blood strength, the greatness, wisdom and knowledge in the glorious mantle of power - and it's for all who will accept it!

Please allow 3-6 weeks for delivery. If you haven't received books in this amount of time, write and let us know, and we will make sure they are sent right away.

IF YOUR BOOKSTORE DOES NOT STOCK THESE BOOKS, ORDER FROM ERNEST ANGLEY MINISTRIES, BOX 1790, AKRON, OHIO 44309
You may also order online at www.ernestangley.org

Name _____

Address _____

City _____

State _____ Zip _____

PLEASE SEND ME THE BOOKS INDICATED:

Qty. ___ B1 - Raptured

Qty. ___ B2 - Faith in God Heals the Sick

Qty. ___ B4 - Untying God's Hands

Qty. ___ B5 - Cell 15

Qty. ___ B6 - God's Rainbow of Promises

Qty. ___ B7 - The Deceit of Lucifer

Qty. ___ B8 - Leeching of the Mind

Qty. ___ B9 - The Power of Bible Fasting

Qty. ___ B10 - Love is the Road

Qty. ___ B11 - Weeds In Eden

Qty. ___ B12 - The Unforgivable Sin

Qty. ___ B13 - Reality of the Blood, Vol.1

Qty. ___ B14 - Prosperity: Spiritual, Physical, Financial...

Qty. ___ B15 - Reality of the Blood, Vol. 2

Qty. ___ B16 - Reality of the Blood, Vol. 3

Qty. ___ B17 - Reality of the Blood, Vol. 4

Qty. ___ B18 - The Reality of the Person of the Holy Spirit, Vol.1

Qty. ___ B19 - The Reality of the Person of the Holy Spirit, Vol.2

Qty. ___ B20 - Hurry Friday

Qty. ___ B22 - The Reality of the Person of the Holy Spirit, Vol.3

Qty. ___ B23 - The Mind of Christ

Qty. ___ B24 - The Reality of the Person of the Holy Spirit, Vol.4

Qty. ___ B25 - Living Free From Sin, Vol.1

Amount enclosed $ _____ (Please No C.O.D.s)

**DISTRIBUTORS AND BOOKSTORES ORDER FROM:
WINSTON PRESS, BOX 2091, AKRON, OHIO 44309**